GOODNIGHT SWEETHEART

Goodnight Sweetheart, All my prayers are for you,
Goodnight Sweetheart, I'll be watching o'er you,
Tears and parting may make us forlorn,
But with the dawn, A new day is born (so I'll say)
Goodnight Sweetheart, Sleep will banish sorrow,
Goodnight Sweetheart, Till we meet tomorrow,
Dreams enfold you, In them dear, I'll hold you,
Goodnight Sweetheart, Goodnight.

GOODNIGHT SWEETHEART

Songs and Memories of the
Second World War

FRANK E. HUGGETT

W. H. Allen · London
A Howard & Wyndham Company
1979

Film set in 12/13 point Plantin
Printed and bound in Great Britain
by W & J Mackay Limited Chatham
for the Publishers, W. H. Allen & Co. Ltd.,
44 Hill Street, London W1X 8LB

Book Design by Bob Hook

ISBN 0 491 02308 1

CONTENTS

AUTHOR'S NOTE

THE popular songs of the Second World War are one of the most neglected aspects of its history, yet for millions of ordinary men and women living at the time they were of supreme importance in sustaining morale, in helping to identify and to express feelings, and in providing much-needed relaxation and entertainment. Their impact was so great that even now there is almost nothing else which can recapture so precisely the atmosphere of wartime and all its changing moods.

In the writing of this book I have made extensive use of many people's recollections of those songs and associated feelings, events and incidents. A brief letter of mine appealing for reminiscences which was published in a number of newspapers and magazines produced an astonishingly large response from both men and women whose feelings about their personal experiences of wartime still clamoured for some public expression. In aggregate, the picture which emerged was so different from many of the stock images that it provided a refreshingly different view of some of the most unexplored aspects of wartime Britain.

INTRODUCTION

FOR every generation the popular songs of its youth have a perennial appeal, recalling those sunny days when the feelings were still warm and unclouded by suspicion or disillusion; but for millions of people who lived through the Second World War, the songs of 1939 to 1945 have a special meaning that they will never lose. Most of the men and women who replied to a letter of mine appealing for song-memories of the Second World War, a letter which was published in various newspapers and magazines, agree that the majority of wartime songs were not of a particularly high standard; but some of them such as *We'll Meet Again, A Nightingale Sang in Berkeley Square, Lilli Marlene, The White Cliffs of Dover, The Anniversary Waltz* and many more are engraved so indelibly by the pressure of personal association upon the memory that even now some people find the recollections they evoke too poignant to bear with equanimity. There are still many people like Mrs Worrod of Birmingham who find it too personally distressing to sing or to hear those wartime songs again. She writes of the present day: 'I have often begun to sing one of those songs whilst working, but halfway through I choke and I have to stop because of the memories. . . . I have quite a large collection of Vera Lynn's records, and although I keep saying that I'll put them on one of these days I haven't got around to it yet; but, maybe after having written this, I will force myself to do so and go back nearly forty years in time.' Some people, on the other hand, cannot hear these songs too often as

they bring back fond memories of what was, in spite of all the sadness and the sorrows, the best years of their lives.

For many men and women the wartime years were the richest in emotion and experience that they have ever known. In those six years a vision of a different kind of life opened up for millions of people who had been jettisoned by the pre-war establishment into an ocean of poverty, public indifference and personal humiliation. All at once, their unused skills, their untested abilities, their long-practised fortitude were needed to win a war which the incompetence and the cowardice of the establishment had partly helped to produce. Both men and women discovered new qualities in themselves which would probably have remained totally concealed from them in peacetime. They mixed with people of different classes and nationalities whom they would never otherwise have known; they visited lands of whose existence they had scarcely heard; they accomplished feats which would previously have seemed impossible.

One former member of the Fleet Air Arm who spent the last years of the war working in the headquarters of South-East Asia Command in Ceylon (as it was then) has never forgotten how he was suddenly transported by the exigencies of war to that beautiful, mountainous island, where he felt for the first, and the last, time that he had a small but significant part to play in a momentous struggle which really could affect the fate of nations for decades. But for him, like countless others, 1945 closed the doors for ever on that kind of life and that vision and he returned to his boring civilian job again. Now, once or twice a year at least, he travels down from his office 'somewhere in the Midlands' to the city on the south coast where his wartime adventures started, to drink again among the deaf and indifferent people in the public house which for him is still filled with the sound of his comrades bawling out the chorus of *South of the Border*. To some people, it may seem sad; to many people, sentimental; but in terms of the lost hopes and the vanished visions of unfulfilled middle age, it is understandable.

Nostalgia can sweeten the past with sickly sentiment, and memory can deceive, particularly in details and incidentals, but most of my hundreds of correspondents have surprisingly balanced recollections of the wartime years. They have forgotten neither the pains of loneliness and of prolonged separation, nor the frustrations of individual aims and the lengthy intervals of boredom between bouts of action. Although there is some sentimental yearning for the 'good, old days', particularly among older people who lived through both world wars, the pains and pleasures, the losses and the gains of wartime are neatly juxtaposed in most memories. There was much less of the false sentiment and class divisions of the First World War, with imperious ladies handing out white feathers, Kitchener's accusatory finger and the moralistic command of songs such as *We don't want to lose you (but we think you ought to go)* of 1914, which had helped to make that conflict far more of a generals' (or a

butchers') war. The concept of death or glory had been buried for most people in the squelching mud of Flanders: it was superseded in the Second World War by a maturer sense of duty and of purpose which had made the immediate introduction of conscription and the subsequent welter of controls acceptable, if not entirely welcome.

Vera Lynn at home, 1940.

The Second World War was far more of a people's war, whose devastating effects were felt right here in the blitzed, but still defiant, cities. Although there were some people living in their country 'funk-holes' who never heard a bomb fall in anger, there were far fewer isolated pockets of protection than there had been in the First World War. The impact of the war on the whole of society was draconian and immediate. Two illustrations of these great social changes will suffice. Even before war had been declared, the population of many quiet country towns and cathedral cities had been radically increased. A million school children and half-a-million mothers and young children under the age of five, many of whom came from the worst slum areas in inner cities, were evacuated to these towns in safe areas.

The effect of the war on the kitchen front was also more immediate. Food rationing did not start until the First World War was nearly over, on 1 January 1918; but it began soon after the Second World War started—on 8 January 1940.

As daily life was increasingly robbed of many of its luxuries, certainties and freedoms, people's feelings, as if to compensate for these restrictions, expanded to fill the vacuum. This normally placid and undemonstrative island-race, with its concealed core of compassion and sentiment, which may not have been lost entirely even now,

began to think and to feel more deeply about themselves, and those around them. They questioned, too, the meaning of their existence and thus their thoughts and feelings were more passionate than ever before. For many women who were young then, the war years with their shared emotion, their comradeship, and their sympathy were the happiest of their lives. Miss Edith Lynes, of Edgbaston, Birmingham, who became a nurse in 1944, got much 'happiness, joy and laughter' from looking after air-raid victims and wounded soldiers, making that period the happiest of her life. But as with many other women of a similar age the post-war years failed to fulfil the promise and the hopes of wartime. She is still a nurse but 'a very disenchanted one'.

Above: Sailors in a canteen at a North African port, 1943. Opposite: Anne Shelton, one of the Forces' favourite singers.

Luxury leave, 1940. Ratings enjoying
a rest after lunch in the houseboat,
Puritan.

The songs to which people danced and listened then helped to reinforce their newly-found thoughts and feelings. Wartime songs were concerned primarily with affirmation, hope and yearning: the old pains of separation or the joys of new discovery added a verisimilitude to their often trite and sentimental lyrics. The songs were carried by the air waves everywhere so that they became as much a part of the new sounds of wartime as the sirens' wail, the crack of guns, the crunch of glass, an omnipresent antidote to war which could be appreciated even by the more sophisticated. 'Extraordinary how potent cheap music is', says Amanda to her former husband Elyot as they listen to a 'sentimental romantic little tune' on the terrace of a hotel in Noël Coward's pre-war play *Private Lives*. It was a

sentiment which was to be more and more widely shared as the war progressed on its seemingly interminable course from year to year.

There is nothing that can carry older people back more swiftly to those wartime years than the memory of those songs. The vocalists who sang them, such as Vera Lynn, Gracie Fields, Anne Shelton, Beryl Davis, Sam Browne and Denny Dennis, are still warmly remembered to this day and so are the big-name band leaders such as Ambrose, Geraldo, Joe Loss, Harry Roy, Maurice Winnick, and some thirty or forty more. The majority of those band leaders had established their reputations before 1939, but the war years added a new lustre to their names even though many of their finest players had been conscripted into the Forces. Most of them had been granted fame and fortune by the idle rich in the pre-war years, but they achieved their greatest success and popularity in the midst of a people's war, playing in garrison theatres, factory canteens and hastily-converted aircraft hangars with rows of armchairs or deckchairs up in front for officers and nurses and planks balanced precariously on piles of sandbags for other ranks at the rear. History had added a piquancy to their years of glory for, even though they did not realise it then, those years were to form the climax of most band leaders' performing careers, as the big band sound was to fade away into a muted whimper in the post-war years with their different attitudes, new electronic equipment and a changed social structure.

Their sounds have mainly gone now, though they have been partly restored to a new generation on re-issued discs and cassettes, but the melodies still linger on in older minds, and the tunes and the refrains still spring readily to many lips. When Mrs A. Rogers of Birmingham saw my letter in her local paper she sat down with her husband that very evening to see how many songs they could remember. She wrote to me later sending me a list of about a hundred songs and told me that they had brought back so many memories for her and her husband that they were 'laughing and singing most of the night'. It is hoped that this book will arouse similar recollections, both sweet and sad, for men and women of the same generation and that it will introduce younger people to a world which is stranger than most of them, one hopes, will ever know.

Above: Harry Roy (second from right) after a broadcast to New Zealand Forces in the Middle East. Overleaf: A Sheffield steelworker at home, 1940.

13

CHAPTER 1

ONE DAY WHEN WE WERE YOUNG

BY 1939 everyone acknowledged that war was coming even though no one quite knew where or when; but Tin Pan Alley had turned its back upon the certainty. The composers and publishers of popular music were not entirely to blame for this evasion as, three years earlier, when the Government's policy of appeasement still protected the tender feelings of the German Chancellor from too much public abuse, the Lord Chamberlain had banned a song entitled *Even Hitler had a Mother*. Even if there had been no official ban, it is doubtful whether there would have been many warlike songs: the public wanted to pack up their troubles, something they had been trying unsuccessfully to do ever since the First World War, originally in their old kitbags and then in their slender shopping baskets. Consequently, the popular songs of that last peacetime summer contained no hint of the approaching storm, ranging from the sadly sentimental like that evocative tone-poem *Deep Purple* and *One Day when we Were Young*, which had been

sung by Deanna Durbin in the previous year, to pure escapist fun such as *Chew-Chew-Chew Your Bubble Gum*, which was described by its publisher as 'the craziest of all crazy songs' and which had just been recorded by Ella Fitzgerald. In the last sad days of that magnificent summer, with an August which was one of the driest and hottest ever recorded, couples danced together in the London parks perhaps for the last time at one-night dances which had been provided free by the London County Council (as it then was). In Islington alone, 20,000 people danced in the parks, while all around lay the marks of preparation for war.

Public buildings had been faced with sandbags to shield them from the devastating blast of air raids which were expected to signal the outbreak of war, while slit trenches added a new night-time hazard to many public parks. Down by the Serpentine, Auxiliary Fire Service, or AFS, recruits were being initiated into the mysteries of hoses and couplings with a humorous coarseness

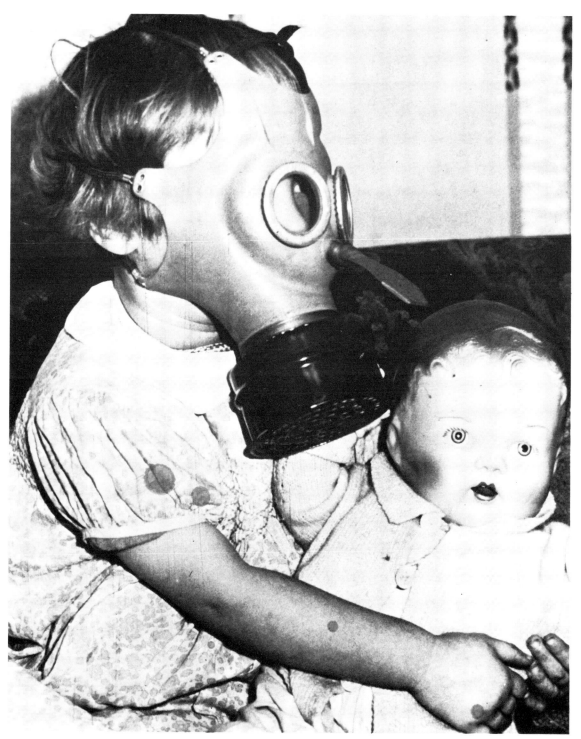

Above: Preparing for war. Overleaf: A pre-war Hunt Ball.

which was to become such a characteristic feature of so much wartime training. ('The male goes inside the female—that's easy enough to remember, ain't it?') Far above them, floating captive in the evening sky, huge silvery barrage balloons, or 'blimps' as they were commonly called, designed to protect the capital from dive-bomber attacks, turned golden-red in the rays of the setting sun.

Throughout the country, thirty-eight million snout-nosed gas masks had already been distributed to all households, where they had been tested, sometimes amidst family hilarity at the sepulchral tones which they added to the normal speaking voice, or at the rude sounds which could be blown through the clammy rubber side-pieces. Back gardens in the inner cities and the suburbs had begun to swell pregnantly with huge mounds of earth which concealed the galvanised steel plates of Anderson shelters, designed to protect up to six people against anything but a direct hit, though not from bronchitis, to which some of their users were later to succumb by spending many hours in their damp, and sometimes waterlogged, interiors. Reservists had already been re-clothed in khaki, while a few women volunteers were also wearing the khaki uniform of the newly-formed Auxiliary Territorial Service, or ATS, with stout black shoes instead of heavier soldier's boots. Many veterans of the First World War had become wardens in the ARP, or Air Raid Precautions, though most of them still lacked the official uniform of brown overalls and were equipped with nothing

Opposite: Ladies chat over tea just before the war.

but a steel helmet, a wooden rattle to warn of gas attacks which never came and a handbell to warn of bombs which eventually did. Within a few months, the uniforms, the organisations and the acronyms which identified them began to multiply.

But most people were far less anxious than they had been during the previous year; they had lived through their worst personal fears and worries during the Munich crisis of 1938 and there was now a much wider acceptance of the inevitable, a growing spirit of resolution, and a determination to make the most of what was sure to be the last few months of peace. In his gossip column in the *Daily Mail* for 5 June 1939, Charles Graves noted that 'the jitters seem now to have almost entirely disappeared', with the unexpected consequence that dentists were inundated with work again for patients who had cancelled their appointments at the time of Munich, thinking that if they were going to an early grave it might as well be with unfilled teeth. The spirit in high society was epitomised by one headline in the *Tatler* in April, 1939: 'On with the Fun, and Blow the Axis!' The article described the re-opening party at the May Fair Hotel, where Sidney Kyte had replaced Ambrose who was touring the variety theatres with an octet; and the pictures showed Princess Natasha Bagration dancing with Prince Obolensky, Miss Jeanne Stuart meditatively smoking a large cigar and the former Peggy Cruise, who had become Mrs John de László, smoking a much smaller cigarette.

In the years between the wars, with all their successive political, financial and international crises, people of all classes had learnt to dance away the 'blues' (one of the songwriters' favourite words), but in different styles, to different tunes and in different places. Members of society danced in exclusive London clubs and hotels where the linen on the circular-topped tables was always spotless, the Dom Perignon and Bollinger were always correctly chilled, and the music was often muted so that it would not disturb the thoughtless chatter of the bright young things or the brooding silences of their elders. Mrs Esmé Strachey, of Iping, Hants, remembers dancing as a young girl at the Ritz where in the middle of the dance floor on hot summer evenings there was a huge block of flower-studded ice to cool the passing dancers. But the crowded floors gave dancers little opportunity to display their skills (even if they possessed any) and most of them were content to 'rhythm dance' with small steps, or to listen to the music or to drown it with their high-pitched gabble. Tunes from the latest stage success of Rodgers and Hart, Gershwin or Jerome Kern were played incessantly, though band leaders could always be persuaded to play a special request for a fiver, or even to give up their place in front of the band to a patron, which usually made little difference to the sound as some of the big-name band leaders were more showmen than musicians. (Billy Cotton, for example, could not read a note of music, and other leaders were indifferent instrumentalists themselves as some of them were too fond of demonstrating at times.)

These London 'niteries', as they were called by young journalists under transatlantic influence, had a virtual monopoly of the services of the best-known dance bands, though a few leaders like Billy Cotton refused to hide his Cockney exuberance and independence beneath the required mask of deference, so that after playing at Ciro's Club for a short time he left for the less pretentious atmosphere of the palais and the variety stage. The names of some band leaders, however, became as closely coupled with particular tunes as their signature tunes with their own surnames. Who, among older people, will ever forget the velvet-smooth touch of the classically-trained pianist Carroll Gibbons playing his signature tune *On the Air* as he introduced another broadcast in his husky Massachusetts drawl from the Savoy Hotel? Sidney Lipton had a long residency at the Grosvenor House Hotel, while Jack Jackson played at the Dorchester Hotel from 1933 until just before the outbreak of the war when his place was taken by Maurice Winnick. But most of the big-name bands, like the music, went round and round, from one hotel to a night club and back again to the same, or a different, hotel.

The big London hotels were open to anyone who could afford to pay, which included English aristocrats and rich foreigners who sometimes brought their own retinue of maids with them who were accommodated at the Dorchester in what were always called the 'couriers' rooms'. The pre-war charges at the Dorchester now seem quite modest. Just before the war, a dinner dance cost 21s., while a bottle of Bollinger cost 22s. 6d. and a 1929 chateau-bottled claret, a mere 8s. 6d.; but the average wage in those days was only about £3 a week. The restaurant, which could seat about 100

people, opened out, in those days when the air was less heavily polluted by the fumes of motor vehicles, on to an open terrace on the Park Lane side; while, on the other, it could be extended for gala nights by removing the high partition screens. There was also a more spacious main ballroom, which is still very much as it was then, with the walls shimmering like an early-morning lake with light reflected from the crystal chandeliers attached to the mirrors on the wall, though the predominant colour scheme was not blue as it is now, but beige in pre-war days. Beige, one of the favourite colours of the Art Deco period, was chosen so that it would not clash with the ladies' brightly-coloured gowns of green, blue and rose, which were the most fashionable colours for evening wear in the Thirties. All the men, of course, wore evening dress, with only an occasional buttonhole to add a splash of needed colour to their black and white uniformity. The air was redolent with the characteristic smells of high society in the Thirties—Havana cigars, Turkish cigarettes and heavy perfumes which had begun to supplant the lighter floral scents from the beginning of the previous decade.

Hotels and restaurants had to close their doors at 2 a.m. but the dancing could go on until early dawn at one of the many night clubs such as the Nut House, the Nest Club or the Bag o' Nails (which housed the No. 1 Rhythm Club later in the war). On the small dance floors, the bright young things could do the night-club shuffle until 4 or 5 a.m., or jitterbug to hot music provided by musicians from big-name bands who had just been released from their metronome

A pre-war dinner in a London hotel.

existence in the grand hotels. The night clubs stayed open illegally, so that there were frequent dawn raids by the police which would be greeted by the dancing debs with shrill shrieks of outraged delight at this welcome diversion in their monotonous life. The only penalty was a free ride to the nearest police station and a small fine. To circumvent the licensing laws, bottle parties were started in the Thirties, where in theory customers bought their own drinks in advance from a wine merchant; but many of them came to grief when they unsuspectingly sold drink to a plain-clothes policeman.

There were also many fabulous private parties in those days when Mayfair was largely residential and still played host to the international set. In June, 1939, for example, an American millionairess, Mrs R. W. van Rensselar, who lived in Park Street, Mayfair, took over the Hurlingham Club for the night to give a party for her niece, the daughter of a French general. One of society's darlings, Jack Harris, and his band, was engaged for the night and a special ballroom was constructed over the lawns to accommodate the 500 guests. The floodlighting, the floral decorations, and the flow of champagne were personally supervised by the six-foot-tall American hostess. Life in those carefree days could be one long party for anyone with the right accent, the correct connections and an easy conscience.

The dancing had to stop much earlier in Hammersmith where the first palais de danse had been opened on 28 October 1919. A poster advertising the opening of the palais proudly proclaimed that it had a sprung maple floor, forty dance instructresses, opulent powder rooms, uniformed attendants—and 'two world-famous jazz bands at each session'. As the passion for dancing spread, huge ballrooms of a similar kind were opened in all parts of the country, so that long before 1939, there was at least one in each of the main cities, such as the Ritz in Manchester, the Plaza in Derby and Green's Playhouse Ballroom in Glasgow. These ballrooms, like the new cinemas of the Thirties, were the harbingers of the mass entertainment age, vast fun palaces for the people where the soft lights and the sweet music could banish reality for a few brief hours and allow dreams and fantasies to flourish. All the skills of modern design were employed to attract people into their warm and comforting interiors, with vast sheets of plate glass and long stretches of chrome glinting under the bright lights in the foyer. In contrast, many of the most exclusive London clubs, which needed no public advertisement of their existence, were approached, like the Embassy Club, along a narrow, rather mean, passage between two shops. Society people went to night spots to chatter and to be seen by people they already knew. Ordinary people, on the other hand, went to the palais to make contact with strangers and to dance, or, occasionally, as Billy Cotton discovered to his surprise when he started playing at the Astoria Ballroom in Charing Cross Road in 1928, just to call out requests for tunes, as teenagers were to do at pop concerts forty years later on.

A night at the palais was not particularly cheap. There were usually two sessions from 3 p.m. to 6 p.m. and from 8 p.m. to midnight, when the admission charge was five shillings against sixpence for a stalls seat in the

Wigan lads and lasses at the Empress
Hall, 1939.

neighbouring cinema. The dancers were predominantly young and members of the lower middle classes or of the more affluent section of the working classes. The men were smartly dressed in their fifty-shilling suits, with their trousers supported by braces and their socks by suspenders, with their hair carefully patted into place with Brylcreem. The girls sat at little tables by the dance floor, (except at Green's in Glasgow where there were tables only in the balcony), their lips and cheeks aflame with the latest shade of brightly-coloured lipstick and rouge. Sequins glittered on their dancing shoes and their evening clutch bag. Short men learnt to judge the height of a girl from her sitting posture to save themselves from the embarrassment of being dwarfed even further by a very tall partner. As they danced, friends would whisper into each other's ears or croon the words of the tune; while strangers could always try the much-used gambit of 'Do you come here often?'

Many of the customers were expert dancers who had mastered the intricacies of ballroom steps at one of the schools of dancing which flourished everywhere in the years between the wars. The programme at the palais allowed them to display their skills. In addition to the regular nights with their waltzes, foxtrots, quick-steps and tangos, there were Latin American nights for those who could do the rumba and the samba and old-time nights for those dancers who preferred the polka, the valeta, the lancers and the old-fashioned waltz. The evening's entertainment was organised with brisk efficiency by the MCs in their eleven-guinea dress suits. They helped to stimulate the spirit of democratic conviviality which was to become even more pronounced on the whole of the home front during the Second World War. This togetherness was encouraged even further by the commercially-minded managements who instituted excuse-me foxtrots and the Paul Jones in which concentric circles of men and women revolved around the floor until a pause in the tune of *Here we go gathering Nuts in May* brought them face to face with a new partner. Spot waltzes, with small prizes for the winners, enticed others on to the dance floor where spotlights weaved a restless warp of light, as searchlights with a more serious intent were to do across the night sky only a year or so later.

There were also many community dances, including the conga, the hokey-cokey, and the palais glide in which friends and strangers linked their arms and kicked their legs in time to *Poor Little Angeline*; the *Lambeth Walk* from the smash-hit musical of *Me and My Girl* of 1937; and *Hands, Knees and Boomps-a-Daisy*, which had been

introduced by Annette Mills on the eve of war.

But it was the popular tunes of the day which were played most often. Some of them, like *Deep Purple*, with its twilight memories of a vanished love, had a universal appeal. But there were others like *South of the Border* which appealed more to the masses, even though few of them had had the opportunity then to sample life 'down Mexico Way'. It was still one of the favourite songs among the BEF in France in 1940. These tunes could be heard in many different places and situations. They were whistled, in that untransistorised age, by errand boys

Jack Payne and the BBC dance orchestra at Savoy Hill, 1928.

as they pedalled through the streets; they were sung in working men's clubs where Vera Lynn made her debut as a seven-year-old in mauve bows and white lace, singing for her supper at 7s. 6d. for three songs and 1s. 6d. for an encore; and they were played on the spotlighted cinema organ which rose slowly from the bowels of the stage to entertain with its honeyed tones in the interval between the main film and the supporting feature.

Although the different social classes shared a liking for some of the same popular tunes, there were scarcely any other links between them in those pre-war days when the lounge and the saloon and public bars in public houses still symbolised and helped to perpetuate a real divide, which only started to be bridged in wartime. Very few ordinary fans had much chance of seeing their favourite dance-band play the popular tunes they liked. Jack Hylton had started to tour the variety halls in Britain and on the Continent in the Twenties, and in the following decade a number of the leading bands made provincial tours to keep up their own fortunes and to revive those of the already ailing variety stage. Jack Payne started touring after he had left his post as resident band leader at the BBC in 1932 and Lew Stone, whose crisp sound is among the most admired by present-day dance band enthusiasts, made a provincial tour in 1935 and also did a stint at one of Butlin's new holiday camps. At the outbreak of the war, Jack Jackson, Jack Harris and Ambrose were all making tours of the variety theatres, though for most of the time Ambrose did not employ his full band but only an octet supported by the singer-comedian Max Bacon and the blonde American vocalist,

Evelyn Dall. Some of the big-name bands starred in rather mediocre films, including Harry Roy, 'the King of Hot-cha', in *Everything is Rhythm*, and Henry Hall, who had succeeded Jack Payne at the BBC, in *Music Hath Charms*: but, on the whole, most of the best dance bands were only heard, not seen, by the mass of the people. Most people had to make do with recordings on 78s, which were scratchily reproduced by steel needles on wind-up gramophones, or with the late-night broadcasts from London hotels which were immensely popular among the nine million people

Henry Hall with the BBC dance
orchestra, 1933.

who had a wireless licence in 1939 and the million or so who had none.

With the primitive technology of the pre-war years and the unshared experiences, values and ambitions, the mass entertainment industry was still in its infancy; but the shared emotions and the common situations and predicaments of wartime encouraged its development so that many popular songs widened their appeal to include most age groups and a wider range of social classes. But in the first few days of official panic following the outbreak of war, the whole of the mass entertainment industry was temporarily obliterated. The television service, which had only 20,000 viewers then, was suspended for the duration, and the regional and national radio programmes were merged into a single Home Service so that enemy bombers could not home in on the transmitters. Dance halls, cinemas, theatres and clubs were all closed by official order to protect the civilian population from the expected blitz which, however, did not come—just then.

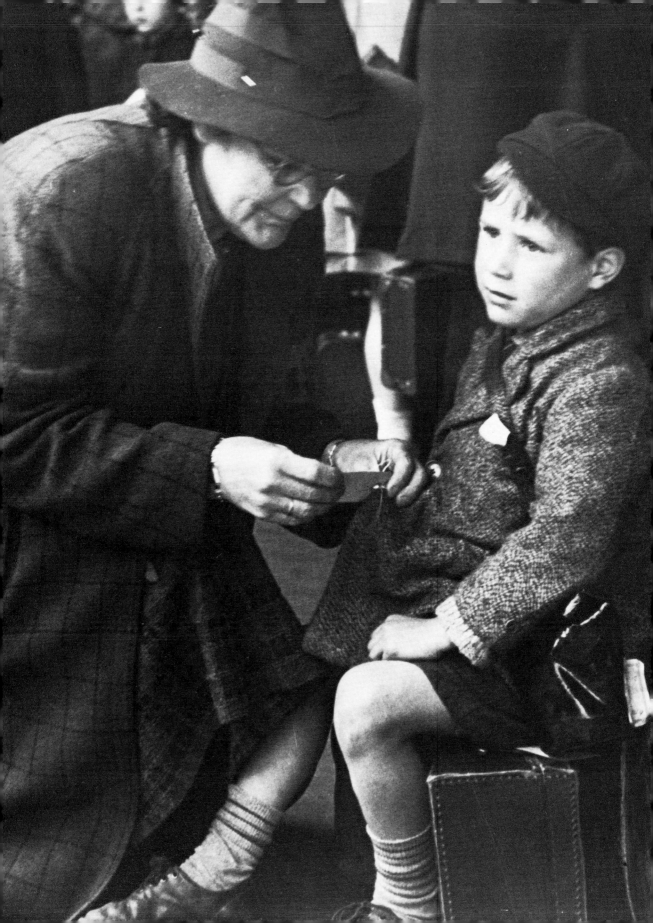

CHAPTER 2

WISH ME LUCK (AS YOU WAVE ME GOODBYE)

T HE majority of servicemen and civilians did not view the war in terms of grand strategy or geopolitical design, but in human terms: it was the impact of remote, impersonal decisions which concerned them and their families. In contrast to the previous conflict with its static slaughter of the trenches and its protected home population, the Second World War was a war of movement and of danger for both civilians and the Forces. In the whole of the nation's history there had never been so many farewells, so many broken families and such vast disturbances of the population. Between 1939 and 1945 there were sixty million changes of address in England and Wales among the civilian population of about thirty-eight million and countless millions more among Servicemen and women who were sometimes moved from one camp to another and back to the original camp again in what appeared to them to be an illogical game of logistics. By early 1940, before the Blitz began, London was estimated to have lost 27 per cent. of its

population, Essex 16 per cent., and Kent 11 per cent.; while Buckinghamshire had increased its population by 35 per cent., Berkshire by 30 per cent. and Cornwall by 17 per cent. There was scarcely a family in the whole land which could remain totally united.

Even before the war began, an estimated two million people, most of whom were rich but who also included some working class wives, had fled to private funk-holes in the countryside where many of them remained for the duration. But the first big, officially-controlled movement of whole segments of the population started on Friday, 1 September, two days before war was declared, when expectant mothers, mothers with young children, schoolchildren and their teachers, and some of the handicapped were evacuated. Every railway station was packed with crowds of labelled schoolchildren, clutching their gas mask in its cardboard case and a small suitcase, often battered and tied with string or straps, which contained most of their worldly

Evacuees are welcomed with strong,
open arms.

possessions. Within four days, over a million schoolchildren and nearly half-a-million mothers with children under five had been transferred from their houses in the threatened cities to billets in private houses in the safer reception areas.

This first evacuation was for many people short-lived; when the bombs failed to fall, they returned to their still unbombed homes in the cities. By Christmas, about half of the schoolchildren had gone back and there had been an even more dramatic decline in the number of mothers and young children in the reception areas, where only 57,000 of the original half-a-million remained. Evacuation provided the first of the many great collective experiences, which were to make the wartime years so momentous in the memory, transforming thousands of middle-class housewives into temporary landladies and dumping city kids from some of the worst slums in inner cities into an alien, and sometimes hostile, environment in the countryside.

The separation of millions of mothers and fathers from their children produced one of the first really popular songs of the phoney war in *Goodnight, Children, Everywhere*. Although the words may now seem excessively sentimental, or even banal, they moved many people deeply then when so many families had been wrenched apart. The song's success was created in part by the occasion and its singer, Gracie Fields, the former mill girl, who was already popular among men and women of different classes, having been accorded the full-page photo-treatment in the *Tatler*, which was more usually reserved for royalty and members of society. She included it in her Christmas concerts for the RAF in France which were also broadcast to listeners back home. As she appealed to her audience in France to join in 'a song for your own kiddies', the men started to sing, shyly at first and then with increased fervour as they realised that in spite of widespread hopes, Chistmas had come but there was still no chance of peace or of reunion with their wives and children. According to a *Sunday Chronicle* reporter, one airman near him couldn't sing as he was doing his best to choke back his tears. Many children were affected in a similar way. Mrs G. Tyszkiewicz, of Birmingham, who was evacuated as a ten-year-old to a place 'somewhere in Wales', says that she and her friends were a really 'rough, tough bunch of city kids,' who used to sing:

We are the Brummagen kids (Repeat)
We know our manners,
We spend our tanners,
We are respected (some hopes)
Wherever we may go.

But whenever she heard *Goodnight, Children, Everywhere*, she felt 'very sad'. Many other children, separated from their parents were brought close to tears by the same song.

After the women and the children, it was the turn of the men to go. The day after war was declared, all fit men between the ages of eighteen and forty were made liable to conscription, unless they were in one of the reserved occupations which then included teaching, mining and instrument making, though the number of reserved occupations was drastically curtailed later on when men and women were selected on an individual basis. By Christmas,

1939, nearly three-quarters of a million men had been conscripted while others had volunteered often to ensure that they served in the more prestigious RAF or Navy instead of the Army. Not everyone was unhappy to leave home. Some men were glad to escape from nagging wives, onerous family responsibilities, unemployment or dead-end jobs; but the majority, torn away from familiarity to face a lonely and uncertain future, were unhappy to depart, particularly those who had just been married. In August and September, clergymen and officials in register offices had been rushed off their feet as couples sought to introduce some personal stability into their lives to counteract what the *Tatler* characteristically called the 'current spot of bother'; while others with a more mercenary eye brought their wedding day forward so that their brides could claim a marriage allowance from the Services, even though for most women it amounted to no more than a miserable £1 or so a week. The number of marriages continued to increase until 1941 as thousands of men and women got three or four days compassionate leave—or what the Forces called 'passionate leave'—so that they could have one lovely weekend before they were posted overseas.

These imposed partings and unnatural separations, which are still what many women and some men remember most from the wartime years, gave Gracie Fields another big success with *Wish Me Luck (As You Wave me Goodbye)* even though in origin the song had nothing to do with the war. Mr N. D. Moore, of Oldbury, West Midlands, a lifelong fan of 'Our Gracie', whom he first saw in 1937 by waiting for four hours to

Our Gracie entertains
the troops.

get a sixpenny seat in the 'unbookables' at the Hippodrome, still remembers her singing it in the film *Shipyard Sally*, which was released in August, 1939. In the film, Gracie Fields played the part of a publican. She sang the song just before she went off to London to fight a brewer who wanted to take over her pub; but the song's cheery message, delivered in her inimitable style, seemed just as relevant

Cross-swords for a RNVR wedding,
1940.

Wrens lend a hand when a Wren
driver marries a naval officer, 1943.

to the thousands of men and women who were saying what might be their last farewells on doorsteps, at barrack gates, through the lattice barriers at railway stations, or at the very end of platforms just before they sloped down to the rails.

Some of the early partings of the phoney war were not without their humorous aspects. 'Every time I hear the song *Wish Me Luck (As You Wave me Goodbye)*,' writes 'Music Lover' of Manchester, 'I have a laugh and think of the day war broke out. My husband and his two brothers were in the Terriers so they were called up straight away. Off they marched in full Royal Signals uniform. His family were all at the gate in tears, waving them goodbye, as though they were going to the ends of the earth. What a laugh it was when they came back the same night. They had only been as far as Bury'—nine miles away.

Later in the war a parting from a boy-friend at a railway station caused a Birmingham lady to smile, as it still does. 'My friend and I were working at a button factory and going out with two soldiers. They were due to go back off leave on the Tuesday. Our excuse to get two hours off work was for me to go to the "dentist" and for my friend to come to "hold my hand".'

'There we were at the station with our friends, while the porter whistled *I'll be seeing You*. With tears in our eyes, we said our last farewells. We turned to go out of the station and bumped into our foreman who was seeing his son off on the same train. *I'll be seeing You* was very appropriate. We got the sack!'

Tender scenes of farewell at railway stations.

*I'll be seeing you
In all the old familiar places
That my heart and mind embraces
All day through.*

But as the war progressed and the needs of individuals became ever more subservient to the impersonal dictates of the war machine, there were some cruel separations which seem even crueller in retrospect. Mrs Alice E. Wilby of Birmingham, writes: 'My husband was in the Army and was given ten days' leave because I was expecting a baby. On the tenth night, in April, when he was due to go back, I was taken in labour. He was determined not to go back and leave me until I had the baby. Next morning, two Redcaps called. The midwife told them to wait a while. Half-an-hour later, as my daughter was born, one of the Redcaps was whistling "I'll remember April, and I'll smile". I lay and heard the tramp of the army boots going down the road, wondering when I would ever see my husband again.'

Another very popular song of the phoney war was *Somewhere in France with You* about the lonely, but uncomplaining girl back home whose thoughts and conversation were always centred on her loved one overseas. Mr Alfred E. Bruce, of Manchester, an ex-regular soldier who had served with the Lancashire Fusiliers pre-war from Palestine to Peking, recalls that the song was very popular with the BEF in 1939. 'Every time I sang it', he writes, 'it brought a lump into my throat; in fact, it still does.'

One short little song which was published in October, 1939, was destined

Opposite: There were even sadder reunions when the wounded returned.

40

to become one of the most popular of the whole war. *We'll Meet Again* was written by Ross Parker and Hughie Charles, one of the most successful and professional wartime songwriting teams. Hughie Charles, who is now seventy-one, says that like all their compositions it was a real team effort: they wrote both words and music together. The song was performed by many thousands of vocalists, both amateur and professional during the war, though it was most closely associated with Vera Lynn, the 'Forces Sweetheart' who made it all her own. It epitomised the feelings of the wartime generation filling millions of civilians in uniform and their wives with hopes of a safe reunion at some unspecified time and place.

We'll meet again, don't know where,
  Don't know when,
But I know we'll meet again some sunny
  day,
Keep smilin' thro' just like you always do
Till the blue skies drive the dark clouds
  far away.

For the unsophisticated these simple songs of hope could express all their most intimate yearnings more readily than they could ever have done themselves; but it was not sentimentality alone that made them so popular. People were conscious then, as they are even more now, of the contrast between these songs' optimistic sentiments and the grim reality of their wartime lives: the irony helped to distance them from events and to make them more bearable. The feelings that these contrasts aroused were so powerful that they became imprinted indelibly upon the memory: the ship that sank with several hundred men while the internal

speakers were playing *We'll Meet Again*; the thousands of men and women with smiles on their faces and that song on their lips who parted lovingly and then wrote a chilling letter later to say that they had found someone else; the men who sang it with such great hope and fervour but never did return. For one former warrant officer, Mr A. G. Pittar, of Crondall, Surrey, the song provided, as it did for millions of others, 'an experience I shall never forget'. He writes:

'Imagine a very large theatre in Le Mans during the phoney war, before Hitler broke through, the theatre packed with Services only, with nurses in their different uniforms, very colourful in their red capes, in the front row of all, then the officers with red cap bands and other ranks behind them. Alone upon the stage, Gracie Fields, in a shimmering dress with a wisp of lace handkerchief which she used with dramatic effect. The song, *We'll Meet Again*: the audience hushed, so that one could nearly hear a pin drop in this huge assembly. I am afraid this song could *not* fulfil the title as very soon afterwards, thousands of young men moved up to the front in their Bren carriers, rattling on the cobblestones through the French villages, to be surrounded and cut off.'

The collective experiences and the shared emotions of wartime gave these songs a widespread appeal by touching a common chord of feeling among male and female civilians of all kinds and classes and among servicemen of rank and those of none. In addition, the Forces had their own favourite songs which appealed to the group rather than the individual and which were more often sung in unison than listened to in reflective silence. Some of the most popular were published early in the war, including *Kiss me Goodnight, Sergeant-Major* (1939), which mocked the lack of domestic comforts and motherly care in the Army;* *Bless 'Em All* (1940), which warned recruits to expect no favours from NCOs of any size or rank;† and *In the Quartermaster's Stores* (1940), which explained why Service grub could never rival home cooking,‡ though in truth it was often more substantial and much more varied, especially for those Servicemen stationed in such countries as South Africa where they could feast on unrationed meat and exotic fruits. These songs, which mocked the hardships of Service life with ironic humour, retained their popularity throughout the war, being sung in crowded canteens, in troopships, in Nissen huts, more often in their bawdy version than their published form.

Another very popular song among both civilians and Service men was *Roll Out the Barrel (The Beer Barrel Polka)* which was published in an English version in May, 1939, but which had ironically first been published five years before in Czechoslovakia, the country which had been sold out to Hitler by the West. Throughout the war its cheerful words and strong beat helped to keep up people's spirits in times of trouble, great and small. It was sung by drunks staggering back home through the blacked-out streets, by civilians trapped by piles of rubble which had been their homes a few hours before, and by the sailors from the *Royal Oak* struggling for survival in the dark, icy waters of Scapa Flow:

Roll out the barrel
We'll have a barrel of fun
Roll out the barrel
We've got the blues on the run.

There was also some place for patriotism in the song-world of the Forces and of civilians. It was expressed in rather sentimental and bucolic terms in *The White Cliffs of Dover*. This song, containing references to shepherds and rather improbable bluebirds, was published in 1941:

There'll be blue birds over
The White Cliffs of Dover
Tomorrow, just you wait and see.
There'll be love and laughter
And peace ever after
Tomorrow, when the world is free.

There'll always be an England written by Ross Parker and Hughie Charles on the eve of war, 'to counteract despair' in the words of Hughie Charles, was another great favourite. But there was scarcely any liking throughout the whole of the war for jingoistic songs. Practically all of those published during the phoney war were failures. Even though *God Bless You, Mr Chamberlain* was described by its publisher as an 'overnight sensation', it failed to win continued public support when it became increasingly apparent that Chamberlain would be no more

* Kiss me goodnight, Sergeant Major
Tuck me in my little wooden bed

† There's many an airman has blighted his life
Thro' writing rude words on the wall,
You'll get no promotion this side of the ocean,
So cheer up, my lads, Bless 'em all.

‡ There were rats, rats
Big as blooming cats
In the quartermaster's stores.

successful in winning the war than he had been in preserving the peace. *Reckless Jeff of the RAF*, another long-forgotten song of the phoney war, seemed inapposite in a period when the main task of air-crews was dropping propaganda leaflets on Germany, while *Oh, ain't it grand to be in the Navy* did little to increase morale in the senior service which had lost its aircraft carrier *Courageous* to U-boats by 17 September and the battleship *Royal Oak* within another month. There was no greater public acclaim for *Berlin—or Bust* or the prophetic *We Won't be Long out There*; while Annette Mills, who wrote the extremely popular *Boomps-a-Daisy*, had much less success with *Adolf*.

The only song of this kind which caught on in a big way during the phoney war was the equally premature *(We're gonna Hang Out) The Washing on the Siegfried Line*, which was one of the few wartime songs to infuriate the Nazi leaders through its bragging contempt for their defensive masterpiece, which they called the West Wall. It was also banned

Two styles of relaxation. Above: RAF crews under training in the US. Opposite: Soldiers in a recreation hut at home.

by some American radio networks before the United States entered the war because it would have infringed their country's policy of neutrality. (After the United States had entered the war in December, 1941, their songwriters found some release for their pent-up passions in such compositions as *Let's Put the Axe to the Axis*, and *We're Going to Find a Fellow who is Yellow and beat him Red, White and Blue*.)

The British people liked the cheeky impudence of *The Siegfried Line* and its encouragement of the sanguine belief that the war could be over by Christmas, 1939; it was one of the first songs to gain a general affection, being sung everywhere from night club to Naafi canteen. Mr W. P. Holt, of Sheffield, who is now in his seventy-eighth year, recalls it being sung when he was sailing across the Channel 'as a member of the 1st Battalion, Royal Scots Fusiliers, anti-tank, known as the suicide squad' to join the BEF in France. They went across under cover of darkness, landing at Cherbourg at 3 a.m. and were then dispersed to Nantes, Le Havre and St Nazaire.

Musical entertainment for ground
crew at an RAF airfield.

ENSA sponsored shows by many well
known bands.

Mr Donald M. Matheson of Sutton
Courtenay, Oxon, has another
song-memory of his sea-crossing to
France. 'I always remember singing *Wish
Me Luck (As You Wave me Goodbye)* as
my regiment left Southampton for
Cherbourg with many of us leaning over
the rails and wondering if and when we
would see England again. How right we
were, as a number of us spent five years as
POWs in Germany and Poland!'
    A few other jingoistic songs had a

slight success. In December, 1940, after the Greeks had surprisingly thrown back the invading Italian armies, *Oh, What a Surprise for the Duce* raised a few wry, appreciative smiles in a blitzed and battered Britain which had still failed to achieve any significant victory on land. In 1943, the novelty number *Der Fuehrer's Face*, written with German 'v's' for English 'w's' and accompanied by the blowing of 'raspberries' right in the Fuehrer's face, had some vulgar success:

Ven der Fuehrer says,
'Ve iss der Master Race'
Ve Heil! Heil!
Right in der Fuehrer's face.
Not to luff der Fuehrer
Iss a great disgrace
So we Heil! Heil
Right in der Fuehrer's face.

The only anti-German song of any merit, Noel Coward's *Don't let's Be beastly to the Germans* was appreciated by the more sophisticated, including Churchill who admired it very much, though the irony restricted more widespread appeal and it was banned initially by the BBC.

There was no necessity for rousing, patriotic songs with a firm beat since, except, in initial training, the Second World War was primarily a mechanised not a marching war. As Major Richard Longland, BBC Liaison Officer with the BEF, wrote in the *BBC Handbook* for 1941: 'In the last war, when the Army marched whenever it had to move, the marching song was something essential. Anything with a good swing was taken up

Noel Coward (right) at a party in an officers' mess of Fighter Command. Overleaf: The Skyrockets Band.

49

and sung on the road and in a few days the whole battalion knew the words. . . . But although an army moving by lorries, tanks, vans and cars doesn't need songs to march to, it still wants songs to sing, and that's why the crooner is popular.'

Nor was there any emotional need for old-style patriotic songs: there was a maturer sense of obligation than there had been in the First World War, a quieter acceptance of a task that had to be done, a deeper attachment to old, but rarely vaunted, loyalties and beliefs. Indeed, there was at first little hatred of the Germans as a whole, though it increased as the struggle became more bitter and prolonged. It reached what is still for some older people an indestructible climax of loathing as tales of the true horror of the Nazi régime and of the widespread involvement of the German nation started to filter out of the concentration camps, particularly Belsen, and out of the occupied countries as they were liberated by the advancing Allied armies towards the end of the European war.

The people's choice of songs, as with much else, was not universally admired, especially by those older members of the establishment who could remember the First World War with its foot-slogging recruits marching cheerfully with a patriotic song on their lips towards the mass slaughter that the establishment had arranged for them but which they themselves did not have to share. In July, 1940, the BBC was still encouraging the writing of 'rousing' songs, and as late as 1942–3 was conducting a campaign against crooning, sentiment and 'slush' on the air. The BBC was deeply divided on this issue. Basically, the argument,

which also raged in other corridors of power, was whether people should have what they wanted, or whether they should be given what the establishment thought would be good for them—the old pre-war division between 'them' and 'us', which was epitomised by one Ministry of Information poster early in the war:

YOUR COURAGE
YOUR CHEERFULNESS
YOUR RESOLUTION
WILL BRING US VICTORY

The old divisions died hard in England, but in the end victory went to the people and it was their voice which was increasingly heard as the establishment was impelled to make some concessions in return for the war effort of the whole people.

The BBC was forced to liven up its broadcasts after there had been much harsh criticism in the Press and in Parliament of the many dull and boring programmes on the Home Service. Before the war, many listeners had expressed their preferences by tuning into the commercial station Radio Luxembourg, which provided the bright and breezy programmes that they liked. That station had been closed down on the outbreak of war: the bored and entertainment-starved men in the BEF started to listen to Radio Fécamp, a French commercial station which broadcast in English, or, even worse, to German stations which also had English programmes. Clearly the BBC had to provide an alternative programme. As Mr B. E. Nicolls, Controller (Programmes) wrote later in the *BBC Year Book* for 1943: 'It was essential that our troops should not feel that the BBC was letting them down by leaving it to other stations to provide the light entertainment that they chiefly wanted.'

To this end, the Director-General of the BBC made a tour of army camps in France to talk to troops and a sample survey of their views was also taken which revealed a great unanimity. 'Most of the demands were for bright, cheerful music and variety', wrote Major Longland, the BBC Liaison Officer, 'stuff that you could beat time to and laugh at and sing with when the winter winds were whistling through the chinks in the barn, and the bleak landscape of north-eastern France was made still more bleak and cheerless by a thick covering of snow.' After some experimental broadcasts a Forces Programme was started in February, 1940, which broadcast twelve hours of mainly light entertainment a day from 11 a.m. to 11 p.m. Introducing the programme Sir Allan Powell, the chairman of the BBC, explained that it was designed to give the troops the kind of entertainment that they wanted, not what others might think it was good for them to hear.

On the whole, the new programme had a good reception among the troops, who wanted something that they could listen to easily and without too much concentration in their crowded canteens and billets. It was what many civilians wanted, too, and far more of them listened to the Forces Programme than to the Home Service. Dance music and popular songs could be heard on every day of the week as the BBC had abolished its pre-war rule of never on Sundays.

Other organisations were even quicker in providing entertainment to keep up the spirits of the troops during the phoney war, with all its boring inactivity on the land and in the air. ENSA, under its redoubtable director, Mr Basil Dean, put on its first concert party starring Frances Day and Arthur Riscoe at Old Dene Camp, Camberley, exactly a week after war had been declared. It was more difficult at first to persuade the military authorities to allow entertainers to go to France. Gracie Fields, who had just undergone a serious operation, was the first to give two concerts to the troops at Douai and Arras in the middle of November, 1939, on her way back to Capri to convalesce. By Christmas 1939, many other top artistes had visited the troops in France and they were followed by some of the big bands, including Jack Hylton, Jack Payne, Joe Loss, Billy Cotton, Ambrose and Carroll Gibbons, who was on holiday in his native America when war was declared and who had fought a one-man battle with the United States authorities to return to the country which he had made his home.

Conscription gradually robbed the big bands of some of their finest musicians; but their loss was the Services' gain. As more and more musicians exchanged their dinner jackets and their £20 or £30 a week for a uniform and two shillings a day, all three Services were enabled to form top-class dance bands of their own. The first, the best and the most famous was the Squadronaires, or the No. 1 RAF Dance Orchestra as it was officially known, whose backbone was a group of volunteers from Ambrose's orchestra. It was led at first by Sgt Leslie Holmes whose stage name was Les Brannelly; and later by Sgt Jimmy Miller, a former vocalist and guitarist with

Ambrose. Their chief rivals were the Skyrockets, or the No. 1 Balloon Centre Dance Orchestra of the RAF, led by Paul Fenoulhet which was also formed in 1940. The Navy had the Blue Mariners under pianist George Crow, while the Army fought back with the RAOC Blue Rockets led by trombonist Eric Tann. In 1942, after there had been some attacks in national newspapers and in parliament on 'tin soldiers' who were alleged to be earning £150 a week, the Blue Rockets was disbanded; but within a few months it had been re-formed and was playing on the air, in army camps and in recording studios again. These bands played too big a part in sustaining morale to be easily sacrificed.

By providing men and women with something from their own world to which they could relate, they helped to keep up the spirits of millions of civilians in uniform and to make Service life a little more enjoyable and tolerable.

Previous page: Four members of the Squadronaires at practice. Above: Four members of the Skyrockets in harmony.

CHAPTER 3

TILL THE LIGHTS OF LONDON SHINE AGAIN

BACK home, on the same day as the first evacuees left for their still secret destinations, the lights went out all over Britain, plunging both city streets and country lanes into Stygian darkness and gloom. In every home, rich or poor, there was a new nightly chore of putting up awkward screens at windows or of drawing heavy curtains which produced a sombre and imprisoned atmosphere in the airless rooms. All street lights and most interior lights in public vehicles were extinguished and private cars were allowed to use only sidelights which had to be heavily masked. Even the lighting of a cigarette in the street could attract the shouted command of an ARP warden or of some officious civilian of 'Put that light out!', the first of the many admonitions with which the civilian population was to be increasingly bombarded on hoardings, in advertisements and by word of mouth.

Almost everyone hated the black-out, though song-writers tried, unsuccessfully, to make people smile at their new tenebrous existence with such

compositions as *The Black Out Stroll, Crash! Bang! I want to go Home* and *Follow the White Line*, whose advice, if it had been taken literally, might well have added to the number of fatal road casualties which almost doubled in the first month of the black-out. Even the more romantic message of *They Can't Black Out the Moon* had little appeal to the young (or older) lovers who were the only ones to welcome the new night-time obscurity with its infinite choice of dark doorways where they could kiss and cuddle.

So great was the general loathing of the black-out that the Government soon introduced some minor relaxations. Civilians were allowed to carry torches in the streets again if the light was diffused by a double sheet of tissue paper. This concession produced one of the first great shortages of the war as torch batteries, particularly the popular No. 8, became extremely scarce, and also some of its first profiteering, as some of the new unbranded batteries expired almost as soon as they were used. Before

Christmas, 1939, most railway carriages were illuminated again with a single, eerie blue light; 'glimmer' or 'star' lighting in city streets cast down a small cone of light at main road intersections: masked traffic lights winked their orders through a small cross; and drivers were allowed to use headlights with blackened reflectors and a paper mask. Early in 1940, metal masks, with slits which cast a dipped ray of light, were made compulsory.

Night and day, there were appalling difficulties in all kinds of travel during the war, though anyone in uniform usually found it easy to thumb a lift from any private motorists who were still on the road. Petrol rationing for the private motorist was introduced on 22 September 1939, with a monthly ration of 4 to 10 gallons of 'Pool' petrol at 1s. 6d. a gallon, and pleasure motoring was abolished altogether, rather tardily, on 1 July 1942, from which date only essential users such as doctors received a small allowance. These restrictions did not affect the mass of people as motor-cars were mainly a middle and upper class luxury then; but the curtailment of public transport did. Many buses were taken off the roads; other services were restricted; and towards the end of 1942 buses stopped running at 9 p.m. in most provincial cities and usually didn't run at all on Sunday mornings.

Difficulties were just as great for the staff as for the passengers, though most of the new wartime 'clippies', who increasingly replaced conductors, managed to preserve a cheery smile. One wartime 'clippie', Mrs Agnes Wearden, of Blackburn, Lancs, writes: 'Whenever I feel low in spirits I sing the wartime song *It's a Lovely Day Tomorrow* which does wonders for me, just as it did in those far-away dark days of the war. I was a bus conductress then, and what with the black-out, the grumbling public, and the awkward hours (I had to be up at 3.30 a.m. to get to the depot for 4.45 a.m.) everything used to get me down from time to time. I'd feel sorry for myself and start weeping and longing for my soldier-husband. Then I'd sing the song, and my burden felt lighter. I'd forget my troubles, as the song says, and learn to say "Tomorrow is a lovely day".'

Rail journeys were even more of a nightmare. Wartime trains were invariably so crowded, slow and dirty that they would make today's worst commuter train seem luxurious. Carriages, corridors, guards' vans, even lavatories, were packed with a swaying, writhing mass of civilians and Servicemen and women encumbered by packs, gas masks, rifles and heavy kit bags sealed with a steel helmet. Only the fortunate, or the pushing, got a seat; the rest had to make do with the minute space that the obstructed corridors allowed. There were hardly any restaurant cars, and station buffets were often closed or impossibly overcrowded. At night, the carriages were fuggy with their closed windows and their drawn blinds and darker than a cinema with their one small blue light. Many people missed their stations, particularly during the invasion scare of 1940, when all road signposts were removed, and the names of railway stations were taken from platforms and replaced by new boards with the names in letters which were only three inches high. Those travellers who did arrive at their right destination were often cold, cramped, hungry and exhausted, as

58

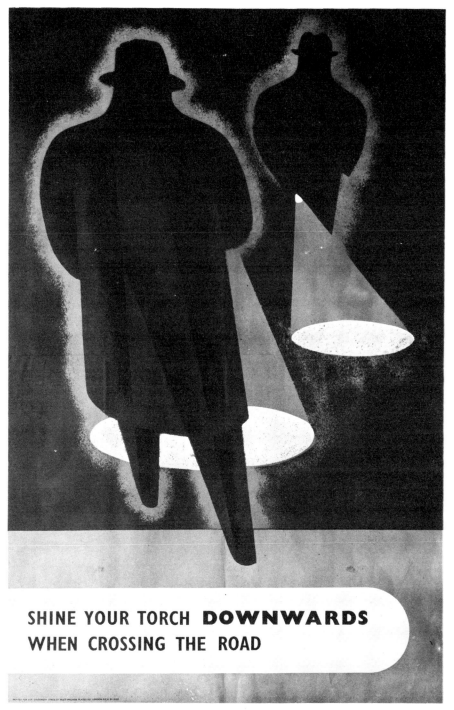

SHINE YOUR TORCH **DOWNWARDS**
WHEN CROSSING THE ROAD

Above: A black-out poster. Overleaf
and following page: There were
crowds everywhere—on railway
stations and in restaurants.

59

delays could sometimes be measured in days rather than in minutes or in hours.

The experiences of van Straten and his band from Quaglino's were worse than most, but not unrepresentative. One Sunday in February, 1940, they set out from London at 10.50 a.m. to give their first provincial concert in Preston. They were due to arrive at 4 p.m.; but at 5 p.m. they were still 500 yards away from Wigan station which they eventually reached three hours later after a series of jolting jerks and shudders. The refreshment room was unheated, and the buffet was closed. They whiled away their seventeen-hour wait by giving an impromptu concert for the 300 other passengers. On Monday, they caught a train to Manchester and they eventually reached London again at 1 a.m. on Tuesday—thirty-eight hours later—to find that no taxis, no buses and no tubes were running.

The cramped conditions and the tedious boredom of most rail journeys encouraged spontaneous conversation and romance. A woman teacher from Yorkshire first became interested in art when she talked for four hours on a wartime train to a private soldier who had been an art critic before the war. Like thousands of other women, Mrs Hilda M. Withenshaw, of Kingsley, Cheshire, met her future husband on a wartime train. He was travelling home from Portsmouth in 1940 on his first seventy-two hour pass from the Fleet Air Arm. She remembers that they had to stand all the way and that he was whistling and singing *The Woodpecker Song*, which was very popular in Britain at that time and also No. 1 in the American hit parade, though it might not have been so popular if more people

had realised that it was in origin an Italian song which had been published there in 1939.

Early in the war, the Government had seriously considered plans to ration rail travel, but such a gross interference with one of the people's few remaining liberties would have been bitterly resented and the plans were abandoned. People preferred to share the egalitarian discomfort of rail travel, but the rationing of food which started on 8 January 1940, with bacon, butter and sugar, was generally welcomed by housewives who were aware that only the rich could benefit if food went 'under the counter'. The popular songs relating to food rationing were light-hearted. *Run, Rabbit, Run!* was written by Noel Gay and Ralph Butler (before food rationing started) for the show *The Little Dog Laughed* which opened in October, 1939; but it seemed even more appropriate later after a meagre meat ration had been introduced on 11 March 1940, when rabbits needed to be even more fleet of foot to escape the farmer's (or the poacher's) gun. Another song, *Hey! Little Hen!*, published in 1941, pleaded with the one surviving chicken to lay an egg for tea, which had become an increasingly rare luxury.

I had a lot of chickens
A large chicken run
But owing to conditions
I'm now down to one.

The song raised a few wry smiles when so many people were feeding kitchen scraps to backyard hens, digging for victory, and trying, later in the war, to make Yorkshire puddings with dried egg. The smiles became less common, however, as rationing was extended to many other kinds of foods and fish, and fruit and vegetables became increasingly scarce so that even the humble onion virtually disappeared for a time. Housewives queued for hours and struggled desperately to avoid mealtime monotony. The Ministry of Food came up with many ingenious, but untempting, recipes for new dishes such as carrot marmalade, carrot flan and Woolton pie, named after the Minister of Food, which consisted of diced potatoes, turnips, the inevitable carrot and any other available vegetable plus brown gravy and a little oatmeal under a pastry crust.

The rationing, the shortages and the general restrictions—a mere foretaste of what was to come—had left people gasping for relief, particularly as the inactivity of the phoney war, whose only battles raged remotely on and below the seas, had made their courage, their cheerfulness and their resolution seem unnecessary and futile. There was just as much official concern about the morale of civilians, particularly of munition workers, as there was about the morale of troops. Many of the jobs in munition factories were boring and monotonous and some of the workers were new to this kind of work. Research in Britain and the United States just before the war had indicated that music could mitigate the strains of working and help to increase productivity. Early in the war, some enlightened managements had introduced their own programmes of music over the factory's internal communications system. Mr Ted Platt, of Belper, Derby, who later served with the RAF, was employed as an assistant inspector of pilots' safety harness early in 1940. 'Before the advent of *Music While You Work*', he writes, 'we had half-an-hour of records played over the internal loudspeaker system. The telephone operator on the factory switchboard (who acted as the DJ) was inundated with various requests, from *The Seigfried Line* to *Umbrella Man*.'

The official *Music While You Work* programme, which was started experimentally by the BBC on 23 June 1940, with mid-morning and mid-afternoon sessions of non-vocal music played by dance bands, light orchestras and military and brass bands, was a tremendous success. A third session at 10.30 p.m. was broadcast for night workers from 2 August 1942. By the end of the war, *Music While You Work* was being listened to by more than four-and-a-half million workers in 8,000 large factories and by a similar number of people in smaller factories and workshops, private homes and Forces canteens. The programme, which was described in the *BBC Year Book* for 1941, as 'an excellent antidote to monotony and boredom, bringing cheer into the gloomiest surroundings and helping to relieve the stress and strain of wartime production,' certainly had beneficial effects on output. In the *BBC Year Book* for 1945, Mr Wynford Reynolds, the programme's organiser, quoted one factory report which said: 'The music exhilarates the workers without acting as a harmful distraction. When the set was shut down for a week, there was a 20 per cent. drop in output.'

Music While You Work was deeply appreciated by millions of war workers. Mrs Jean Stokes, of Northallerton, Yorkshire, worked in a factory during the

Women played a big part in munition
factories.

war making RAF and GI uniforms. She writes: 'Music helped us to get through the long hours of eight to six, also Saturday mornings. *Music While You Work* was played every day, but we also entertained ourselves, singing *Roll Out the Barrel*, Vera Lynn's song *We'll Meet Again* and *Yours*, which was my favourite. I also played the piano during the lunch breaks and the girls always asked me to play *Jealousy*.'

Concerts and community singing were very popular in war factories as singing helped to lift the spirits out of the slough of routine work. Miss Edith Lynes, of Birmingham, remembers how 'two nervous teenagers, me being one of them', sang *The White Cliffs of Dover* and *My Devotion* 'in a canteen at midnight in a shadow factory making the Stirling bomber around 1941 to 1942.' Miss N. Coward, of Poole, Dorset, who also worked in a munitions factory during the war, recollects that community singing helped to keep up their spirits, particularly in wartime crises. 'It gave us a lot of hope', she says. 'After all, we were all in it together.'

Not everyone in authority was filled with personal enthusiasm for communal merrymaking. In July, 1940, Mr Ernest Yates, of the Amateur Musicians' League, suggested to the Ministry of Information that the Aeolian Hall in New Bond Street, of which he was the tenant, might be used in the lunch hour for music and community singing by workers in the distributive trades. In a letter to an MOI colleague, Sir Kenneth (now Lord) Clark, who was then Controller, Home Publicity, MOI, confessed that 'the thought of amateur musicians singing at lunch-time strikes a chill into my heart';

but he conceded that 'such performances might give pleasure and encouragement to quite a number of workers' and sought the advice of Miss Glasgow, of the Council for the Encouragement of Music and the Arts, 'who has plenty of bitter experience of the difficulties involved'.

Other people, however, had fewer doubts, including the Minister of Labour, Mr Ernest Bevin. With his support, ENSA, whose signature tune was *Let the People Sing*, put on the first of its many concerts for war workers at Woolwich Arsenal on 22 July 1940. The BBC followed with *Workers' Playtime*, which was first broadcast from a factory in Wrexham on 31 May 1941, and with *Works Wonders* which gave the workers themselves a chance to display their talent—or lack of it. Visits by well-known dance bands always got an enthusiastic reception in factories. Mrs Jean Stokes says: 'You can imagine the thrill of seeing the famous Joe Loss playing *In the Mood*. We all crowded into one large room; we had to stand on tables, sit on the floor and even the window sills and the stairs. About 300 girls and boys were there, all clapping to *In the Mood*.' Mrs W. Gallagher, of Solihull, who got her first job during the war as a sixteen-year-old girl working in the canteen of a munitions factory, remembers how thrilled she was when Geraldo came to give a concert in the canteen. After they had served the band with lunch, the canteen girls asked Len Camber, one of Geraldo's vocalists, to sing for them. 'We all stood outside the canteen and he sang *Long Ago and Far Away* which was very enchanting and romantic. We talked about it for a long time afterwards and still do when my friends (the same friends but older) and I

A wine bar in Liverpool. Overleaf: 'Cheers!' Sailors and shipworkers, 1941.

meet and think of the happy memories but drab days of long ago.'

Outside the factories, too, it was the traditional attitudes and values of the working classes that came increasingly to predominate—their mateyness, their immediacy, their lack of personal reticence, their ironic sense of humour, their sense of fair play. Because their pre-war life had provided most of them with so few material benefits, they suffered far less deprivation during the war than the middle classes whose world of privilege lay shattered, never to be restored. Some workers were better off financially than they had ever been before, with skilled munition workers reportedly earning £11 a week by 1940, about three or more times the average pre-war wage; and even troops could have a good night out on a few shillings in 1940 when Players cigarettes, medium, mild or cork-tipped, cost sevenpence for ten and a pint of beer cost sixpence.

On 22 August 1940, Sir Kenneth Clark wrote a note to his Minister saying: 'Nearly everyone seems agreed that the Government should not be too openly associated with schemes for communal merry-making, but I think that people should be told by some responsible ministers, if possible by the Prime Minister, that they will not be doing wrong in enjoying themselves and taking advantage of whatever entertainments are offered. . . .' But most working class people, who had long been accustomed to making their own entertainment whenever they had the opportunity or the money to do so, needed no official encouragement to enjoy themselves in their own way.

Pubs, which had long been the solace of the working man and woman, were more crowded than they had ever been. To come in from the gloomy streets with their uniformly blackened windows, whose darkness was temporarily relieved only by the occasional yellow flicker of a masked headlight or an obscured torch, was to enter a warm, noisy world where no one needed to be a stranger for long. Although there were some surly landlords and disgruntled, ugly barmaids (the beautiful barmaid was more a part of folk memory than reality), wartime pubs on the whole were friendly and more welcoming than they have ever been since. Mrs A. Bennett, of Northfield, Birmingham, who is now seventy-five years of age, is just one of the many older people who look back with nostalgia on those distant days when people really were good friends and neighbours. 'My husband and I', she writes, 'used to look forward to our Sunday nights out at the Woodman on the corner of Well Street and Barr Street, Hockley. They were the happiest years of my life. . . . We used to love to go to a pub where there was just a piano playing and we all used to sing together.'

Working men and women had always liked sing-songs. Mr Ted Platt still vividly remembers his last pre-war holiday at Blackpool where he arrived from Birmingham on a new bicycle he had just bought on hire-purchase for two shillings a week. 'At eighteen, it seemed a marvellous place; the holiday atmosphere was terrific, *South of the Border* was the outstanding number of the year. While walking along the prom at nights, there were couples dancing to the music of accordions, plenty of impromptu sing-songs, and also a lot of activity on the beaches. It was the most wonderful place on earth to a young romantic.'

Sing-songs had never been so prolonged or so boisterous as they were in wartime. Miss Evelyn G. Fiford, of Kingswood, Bristol, a graduate who worked as an executive in the Admiralty at Bath, was one of the many pianists who gave their services voluntarily for these nightly get-togethers. She played at pubs, inns and hotels over a wide area, including the Griffin Inn at Wick, Gloucestershire, the Rose and Crown at Warmley, the Swan Inn near the top of Tog Hill in Gloucestershire, the Bull Inn at Downton near Salisbury, the Stag Inn at Britford, Wiltshire, the Follies Inn at Yate, Gloucestershire, and the Pulteney Hotel in Bath—the Admiralty Club. Some of the songs she used to play were *Yours, Run, Rabbit, Run!, London Pride, The White Cliffs of Dover* and some songs from the First World War, including *Keep the Home Fires Burning* and *There's a Long, Long Trail a-Winding*. 'Sometimes a collection was taken', she writes, 'and the money was shared out among people who had lost their jobs after the blitz on Bristol.'

There were also sing-songs in many private homes. Social barriers started to crumble as some middle class families opened up their houses to provide meals, hospitality and entertainment for lonely Servicemen and women—for the duration. Mrs R. Hutchinson, of Malton, Yorks, writes: 'At the time I was in my teens and living with my parents and my sister in the farmhouse. During the war, ours was "open house" to Servicemen stationed in the neighbourhood and also to the numerous families who could come for a week or two of respite from the bombing in the cities. Pre-war, we catered for the Cyclists' Touring and National Cyclists' Clubs; that was how people had our address.

'Many an evening was spent singing and playing on the old piano. Anybody who could play could do so when they wished, and many lonely chaps who didn't want to go to the pub, would come for an evening for threepence—the cost of a sandwich and a cup of tea.'

The song she remembers most is *Whispering Grass* which was being sung in a very high key by a middle-aged lady one night. Her Commando son, who was on embarkation leave, was squatting down by the piano with tears streaming down his face. They were all feeling sorry for him, as they thought he was touched by his mother's singing; but when she had finished and went out of the room for a minute, he burst out laughing. 'They were tears of laughter, not of sadness, as we had imagined. Mind you, we had all felt like laughing really.'

All over the country well-meaning amateurs organised concert parties to provide entertainment, of varying quality, for troops and civilians. Mrs Winifred M. Snowden, of Sinnington, Yorks, remembers how her father formed a concert party to raise money for the Red Cross and other charities, which gave many wartime performances in neighbouring villages. On one occasion, tulips were chosen as the theme for song and, in spite of shortages, her mother made dozens and dozens of paper tulips; someone else made a windmill; and all the performers wore Dutch costume. Mrs U. Stares of Swaythling, Southampton, made her first stage appearance as a ten-year-old during the war, singing and

tap-dancing to *The White Cliffs of Dover* before an audience of wounded soldiers at the General Hospital, as it is now called. 'I can still picture those soldiers today,' she writes, 'swathed in bandages, but smiling and clapping like mad. Later on in the war, I joined a youth club and we toured locally, singing and dancing to all the popular songs of the day.' She and other members of that youth club still have such fond memories of those years that six years ago they formed a Youth Club Reunion Association which meets once a month to dance to the music of the Forties and which also holds a dance every year in the Guildhall,

Southampton. Increasingly in many other parts of the country, too, civilians and associations of Servicemen and former prisoners of war, with nostalgic memories of those years, hold annual wartime dances 'somewhere in England' at which some of the dancers wear uniform or wartime clothes.

Above: Civilians and soldiers get together for a sing-song. Overleaf: The middle classes opened their gardens to Servicemen. Following page: Leg shows provided a different sort of entertainment for the troops.

PRINCE OF WA[LES]

NO MONEY
REFUNDED
NO
RE-ADMISSION

OPEN TILL 10 P.

PRICES of ADMISSION
STALLS AND CIRCLE
IF AVAILABLE

2'6 3'6 4'6

6'- 8'6 10'6

SEATS BOOKABLE IN ADVANCE

6'- 8'6 10'6

ALL INCLUDING TAX •

SPECIAL TERMS
— FOR PARTIES OF OVER TWENTY

DON'T HELP
THE ENEMY!

Professional entertainment was in even greater demand. Within a week or so of the outbreak of the war, the Government had allowed theatres, cinemas and dance halls to open again, though they had to shut by 10 p.m. Revues and stage shows provided their quota of popular wartime songs. At the beginning of the war everyone was whistling and humming *My Heart belongs to Daddy* sung by the dark-haired Pat Kirkwood in *Black Velvet* at the London Hippodrome in November, 1939. Her part was taken over a month or so later by Beryl Davis, the fifteen-year-old daughter of Harry Davis, who had long been associated with Oscar Rabin's Band, one of the favourites of the palais dancers. Just before the end of the war in Europe, everyone was singing *We'll Gather Lilacs* which had been sung by Olive Gilbert and Muriel Barron in Ivor Novello's *Perchance to Dream* in April, 1945, at the same theatre.

Cinemas, which often had long queues stretching right round the block in even the worst weather, had never had it so good: about thirty million tickets were sold every week. Films provided some of the main popular songs, from

Above: Aircrew training in the US had their own camp cinema.
Opposite: Non-stop revues were popular at home.

Over the Rainbow sung by Judy Garland in *The Wizard of Oz* just after the outbreak of war; through that perennial best-seller *White Christmas* sung by Bing Crosby in *Holiday Inn* in 1942; to *The More I see You* sung by Dick Haynes in *The Diamond Horseshoe* just after VJ day. Films also gave fans a chance to see some of the big-name American bands, including Glenn Miller in *Sun Valley Serenade*, Jack Teagarden in *Birth of the Blues*, Gene Krupa in *Ball of Fire* and Jimmy Dorsey in *The Fleet's In*—all in 1942.

One film of 1941, *Dangerous Moonlight*, starring Anton Walbrook as a Polish pianist, was, and still is, remembered mainly for its music. His playing of the *Warsaw Concerto* as the bombs crunched down in the moonlight outside came to symbolise the spirit of resistance to Hitler. 'I can still remember seeing that film', one London housewife writes, 'as if it was yesterday. I was feeling very depressed as my husband was in the desert and I had not heard from him for weeks. My daughter suggested that we should go to the cinema as she knew that I liked Anton Walbrook. I loved the film and although I came out of the cinema in tears, the music made me think that everything was worthwhile.' Mrs R. Hutchinson remembers how a former professional musician in his forties, who used to play the piano at their Friday night 'hops' in the local school, left all his sheet music with her when he was posted overseas with the Pioneer Corps, except for his copy of the *Warsaw Concerto*.

The theme music by Richard Addinsell, which became 'extravagantly popular' as the *Oxford Companion to Music* rather disparagingly remarks, had a great effect on many ordinary people, opening their ears for the first time to a different kind of music. As people's feelings expanded under the experience of war, the appreciation of classical music, which touched deeper levels of emotion, increased considerably. Jack Hylton, the band leader and impresario, had sensed this change of taste early and by August, 1940, had introduced the London Philharmonic Orchestra and the pianist Eileen Joyce to a variety-theatre audience at the Glasgow Empire with great success. Other enterprising managements of variety theatres also started to provide more serious entertainment. The Palace Theatre in Plymouth, for example, put on concerts and ballets with similar success. ENSA, too, started to provide concerts of serious music for the troops, the first being presented at the Garrison Theatre, Aldershot, in October 1940. Later in the war, ENSA also started to present special symphony concerts for war workers with a standard admission charge of a shilling. In spite of all the pessimistic doubts of some of the middle class cultural élite, these too were an enormous success as the separate cultures of peacetime started to crumble and to merge under the pressure of total war.

The first ENSA concert of this kind was given by the Hallé Orchestra under its conductor John Barbirolli at Wigan on 11 October 1943. After one such concert in 1944, Mr Charles J. Bartlett, the managing director of Vauxhall Motors, Luton, wrote to the Director of ENSA congratulating him on the 'tremendous success' which 'was startling in its results not only to the large number of people here, but also to the BBC Orchestra themselves, who were greatly elated at getting such a large, well-behaved and appreciative audience'. These concerts were usually held in any suitable large hall, or church or cathedral, in cities which contained large concentrations of war-workers; but some were also put on in the factories, not amidst the clatter of crockery and cutlery in lunchtime canteens, but in quiet rest rooms or factory halls. The appreciation of classical music was also greatly encouraged by the learned, witty and entertaining talks given by Dobson and Young on the BBC and at many Service camps.

Although the war produced a more catholic taste in music, the people's first love still remained dance music and popular songs. There was an extraordinary boom in dancing in wartime, set off when Joe Loss packed 10,000 customers in a week into Green's Playhouse Ballroom in Glasgow in 1940. Other dance halls all over the country started to do excellent business, with their coffee dances for an hour and a half in the morning, their tea dances for two hours or so in the afternoon, and their evening sessions from 6.30 p.m. to 10 p.m., which was extended to 11 p.m. by the Government in February, 1940. Many dance halls admitted members of the Forces for half the normal price and provided them with dancing shoes, free of charge, to protect their precious, irreplaceable floors from the heavy pounding of army boots. Some managers had a Forces-only night once a week, when ladies, but no male civilians were admitted.

As in many other spheres of life, women started to play a much bigger part as men were conscripted into the Forces. In October, 1939, Mrs Jack Hylton, who had been a dance band leader for many years, tried to form an all-girls' band, but she had to abandon the attempt as it proved impossible to get suitable trombonists and trumpet players. Ivy Benson experienced the same initial difficulty when she tried to form an all-girls' band. Of the two trombonists who offered their services one was sixty-nine and the other fifty-four and neither of them wanted to undertake arduous provincial tours. But by February, 1940, she had formed a ten-piece ladies' band which opened in a revue called *Meet the Girls* at the Norwich Hippodrome.

Although her band provoked some professional jealousy among male musicians, it was very popular with members of the public, both male and female. Mrs Mary Holbrook, of Washington, Tyne and Wear, recalls how Ivy Benson and her band provided the weekly highspot of her life when she was working with other girls from Durham in the BSA factory in Birmingham. 'We had to do twelve hours' permanent night shift', she writes, 'to let the local women be home at nights with their children, as we got a lot of bombing. Wednesdays, though, were different. We used to get to bed early; then in the afternoons go out to the Bull Ring, to the tea dance with Ivy Benson and her all-girls' band. Those were really happy days.' After playing at various provincial dance halls, including the Ritz Ballroom, Manchester and the Locarno, Glasgow, Ivy Benson and her band moved to London just before Christmas, 1941. A year later, it became one of the resident BBC dance bands.

Henry Hall with vocalist
at Green's Playhouse, Glasgow,
1944.

Knitting for victory at 'The Peggy
Bedford', Longford. Overleaf:
Soldiers on leave from France had an
enraptured audience.

Other all-girls' bands were led by Blanche
Coleman, Gloria Faye and Tony
Heaton-Parker, who had played the
drums with Ivy Benson, but none became
so famous.

During the first months of the
phoney war a few new dance halls were
opened and many other places of
entertainment were converted for the
duration. The Dome at Brighton, for
example, was given over to dances and
Sunday afternoon concerts for the
Forces, while Servicemen and specially
invited contingents of girls from big
London stores danced in the Royal
Opera House, Covent Garden, where
Beniamino Gigli, the Italian tenor, and
Germaine Lubin, the French soprano,
had sung in the last season before the
war.

The transformation of opera house
into dance hall was symbolic of the
wartime change of values. Even if it had
been possible to mount lavish and
expensive spectacles for a cultural
minority, it would have been politically
unacceptable in wartime Britain.
Although there were many exceptions
and anomalies, the British fought a public
war in which all people were expected to
share, and to show, their sufferings. In
contrast, the war on the Continent, even
before the occupation, had been much
more of a private war fought in the
conscience between the extremes of
resistance and collaboration.

The openness in Britain did produce
a great unity and strength of purpose,
which gave the country its 'finest hour'.
The ultimate issues and the immense
resolve were rarely discussed openly,
which deceived many American observers
about the true nature of British feelings
during the phoney war, as they watched a
nation drink and dance the nights away in
apparent unconcern. But the blitz soon
showed that their analysis had been
wrong.

CHAPTER 4

A NIGHTINGALE SANG IN BERKELEY SQUARE

HE phoney war ended abruptly, and the real war on the Western Front began, at 3 a.m. on 10 May 1940, when the Germans launched an attack on the Netherlands and Belgium. The Netherlands was overrun and conquered within five days, and the Belgium king capitulated thirteen days later. During the next few weeks the BEF, fighting desperate rearguard actions, was forced back to a narrow bridgehead on the French coast near Dunkirk, where nearly 350,000 British and allied troops were evacuated to England many of them by small craft, fishing smacks and pleasure steamers. The fighting still went on in France; but by 14 June the Germans had taken Paris and six days later the new French Government under Marshal Pétain had asked for an armistice. Meanwhile another 130,000 British troops had been evacuated from other French ports.

Scarcely had the defeated troops returned home than what Goering boasted would be the final assault on Britain, started from the skies. The first

concentrated air-raids began during the Battle of Britain in July, 1940, and they became more severe in August when over a thousand civilians were killed; but the real blitz started on Saturday, 7 September 1940, when the East End of London was bombed for the first time. For more than two months there were continuous air-raids, night after night, on the capital, and these continued with only occasional intermissions while provincial cities bore the main brunt of the German attacks until 11 May 1941, when the last major air-raid was made on London.

The blitz produced no great songs of resolution or defiance, only a few anticipatory songs such as *When they Sound the Last All Clear*—a trite formula which was to be endlessly repeated through the war from *Till the Lights of London Shine Again* of 1940, through *I'm going to get lit up (When the Lights Go up in London)* of 1943 to *Shine on Victory Moon* of 1944. Indeed, very few boastful or cheery patriotic songs were written after Dunkirk, a major defeat which British ingenuity and bravery, and Hitler's

A kiss for a soldier back from Dunkirk. Overleaf:
Good food could still be obtained—at a price.

misjudgment, had turned into a partial victory. Instead, the music publishers, sensing that the public needed reassurance, thumbed through their old files, as they sometimes do, and came up with many revivals, including *The Best Things in Life are Free* of 1928, *Sleepy Lagoon* of 1931 and *If I Had My Way* which had originally been written in 1913.

Some of the new songs also gained their popularity through their assurance that there had been better times such as *The Last Time I saw Paris* and *A Nightingale Sang in Berkeley Square*, which became for many people, particularly the middle classes, the song of the blitz.

The streets of town were paved with stars
It was such a romantic affair
And as we kiss'd and said 'goodnight',
A nightingale sang in Berkeley Square.

The song had become an overnight success before the blitz began when it was sung by Judy Campbell in the revue *New Faces* in June, 1940. For those who saw the show, the memory of that attractive brunette with high cheekbones, singing dreamily in lacy white of her Mayfair romance brought back fond memories of those vanished times when the dawn was truly 'gold and blue' and not blackened by the thick pall of mauve and orange smoke which towered daily above the still burning buildings. Ironically, the windows of flats and offices in Berkeley Square were shattered only ten days after the blitz began. The song was played endlessly at dances, whistled in the streets, and sung by other vocalists from stages of variety theatres in all parts of the country. Mr George W. Self, of Alton,

Hants, can 'still see a slim young man singing this song on a theatre stage in Portsmouth', while devastation lay all around outside.

Even during the blitz, the old pre-war life of privilege for the rich minority persisted in the West End, scarcely changed in outer form and not much more in inner substance. An article, 'I'm Just Back from Town', which appeared in the July, 1941, issue of *Vogue*, said: 'George and I had a really swell evening, starting off with drinks at the Ritz, and more at the Dorchester, and then eats at the Causerie, the newish place at Claridges—it's always packed out. There's a sumptuous centre buffet, simply groaning with the most lush *hors d'oeuvres*, and you're let loose on it, with a plate and fork. There were lots of women in uniform, looking incredibly spick and span and soignée . . . how *do* they do it? Yes, we made quite a night of it, and fetched up at the Suivi, round about 2 a.m.' The luxury hotels, the restaurants and the clubs in the West End were still packed nightly with the same old crowds, including bemonocled men and cigar-smoking women, though most of the men had now exchanged their pre-war uniform of black and white for another of light or dark blue or khaki and there was also a new kind of customer whose wallet bulged with black-market notes.

Ralph Ingersoll, the American author of *Report on England* (1941), found scarcely any changes in the luxury hotels. Customers were rationed to three lumps of sugar per meal, but the granulated sugar still flowed freely from the silver-topped shakers, while the lunch menus and the wine lists seemed to be as bountiful as those in hotels of countries which were not at war. But on reflection, he realised that the meals were not perhaps quite so good, and the service also was less efficient than it had once been, a development which he attributed to the internment of Italian waiters.

Night clubs and bottle parties flourished, even though they were more frequently raided by the police, disappearing and re-appearing with their old pre-war vitality with new ones rising phoenix-like on the ashes of the old, as Le Suivi had done on the site of the Old Stratton Club in January, 1940. Some of the best-known night spots in wartime London were the Cabaret Club in Beak Street, the Cotton Club in Denman Street, the Four Hundred in Leicester Square, the Nut House and the Slip In both in Regent Street.

When the first bombs fell on London, the West End went on dining and dancing, apparently unconcerned. Sidney Lipton continued to play on as usual until 12.30 a.m. at the Grosvenor House Hotel, while Norman Cole went on until 1 a.m. at the Piccadilly, when customers who were unable to find a taxi to take them home booked a room at the hotel and stayed for the night. Within a few days, however, those clubs and restaurants which had not made arrangements to go underground, had to close. People could no longer dance to the music of Harry Roy at the Café Anglais or to the music of George Melachrino at the Embassy Club, or listen to Felix Mendelssohn and his Hawaiian Serenaders in the restaurant at Madame Tussaud's. But some clubs and restaurants survived, like the Martinez off Regent Street where the jollity still

went on in the wine vaults in the cellar.

The luxury hotels, which were even better prepared for the blitz, provided better facilities for their distinguished clientele. Although there were still no angels dining at the Ritz, where a room then cost £5 a night, it did provide a haven, according to the *Sunday Express* of 8 September 1940, for ex-King Zog of Albania, ex-Queen Geraldine and twenty-eight members of his suite. The same newspaper reported that there were nine peers, including the Halifaxes and the Duff Coopers, living in the Dorchester. Patrons no longer dined in the restaurant overlooking Park Lane, which was sheltered by nothing more substantial than a roof garden, but in the inner oval ballroom-lounge, which was protected by the whole of the reinforced concrete structure; while society ladies could be pummelled into shape for their war effort in a 'spa' or health bath twelve feet underground. Just up the road, at the Grosvenor House Hotel, diners had moved into the safety of the basement grill-room, while over at the Savoy, Carroll Gibbons and his Orpheans, now reduced from ten pieces to five, played every night in their underground shelter. The Savoy boasted that within three minutes of the sirens sounding (whose 'banshee howlings' in Churchill's expressive phrase had just been reduced from two minutes to one), the six telephone operators at the hotel could summon every guest to the relative safety of mattresses in underground cubicles.

These surviving bastions of pre-war privilege aroused the anger of some militant East Enders, which produced a minor, but socially significant, confrontation in the very heart of the

Above: Many ordinary people spent
their nights in the Tube. Previous
pages: There was a different kind of
nightlife for the rich.

West End. According to the *Daily Worker*, the Dorchester was at first selected for this staged confrontation, but eventually, the Savoy, with its resident American journalists, was chosen instead. Shortly after the sirens sounded at 8 p.m. on Saturday, 14 September 1940, a group of about forty East Enders, led by Councillor Phil Piratin and 'Tubby' Rosen of the Stepney Tenants' Defence League, pushed past the astonished hotel porter, who had never seen anything like this in his life, and demanded shelter in the safety of the hotel. Contemporary reports about what happened next are confused, but all agree that the confrontation ended quickly as, uncharacteristically, the all-clear sounded within half-an-hour giving the manager a chance to usher his uninvited guests from the hotel. For a fortnight afterwards, there were reports of blanket-carrying East Enders waiting outside West End Clubs for the sirens to sound; but there were no reports of other confrontations.

Cockneys from the East End who bore the brunt of the first air-raids were just as militant and more successful in their demands to use the London Underground stations as shelters, which the government had initially resisted, fearing that it might create a shelter psychosis with devastating effects on morale. People evaded the ban by buying a ticket for the Tube and refusing to come out again. By 11 September 2,000 East Enders had encamped for the night in Holborn Station and advance guards of this invading army of the blitzed and the homeless had already infiltrated some stations further west. Within a week, the East Enders, carrying their blankets and sandwiches, had moved into the heart of London, sharing the same tube stations with West Enders, who arrived with their picnic baskets and travelling rugs. An official at one tube station was reported in the *Daily Mirror* of 20 September 1940, to have said that most of them were regulars and that they all got on well together. Faced with such great public pressure, the authorities capitulated and bunk beds, drinking water and canteens were eventually provided in tube stations while Aldwych station was designated as a permanent shelter. It was there, on 8 October, that ENSA provided its first concert party for shelterers; George Formby put on a show for them later which was broadcast. Owners of private deep shelters in the West End also opened their doors to outsiders. One shelter under a block of luxury flats at Marble Arch was regularly used by workers and their wives and by soldiers and their girl friends; they waltzed the night away and did the *Boomps-a-Daisy* to the sounds of a guitar played by Charles Molleman, a refugee engineer from the Belgian Air Force.

On 14 November 1940, the Luftwaffe turned its main attention away from London temporarily to bomb Coventry, using a new technique in which the city centre was first set on fire by incendiaries to act as a beacon for the following waves of bombers which rained down their bombs on the blazing city. All major provincial cities had their share of the bombing. Sheffield had its worse raids on 13 and 15 December 1940; Portsmouth on 10 January and 10 March 1941; Plymouth on 21 and 22 March and on five nights towards the end of April.

Manchester's turn had started on Sunday, 23 December 1940, a night

which still brings back vivid memories for Mrs Winifred E. Hughes, of Bramhall, Cheshire. She was thirteen at the time and used to go with her brother Bill and other friends in their youth club to the big band concerts at Hulme Hippodrome on Sunday nights. The vocalist had almost finished singing *Begin the Beguine* when the manager came on stage to announce that there was an air-raid and that the Hippodrome had been hit by an incendiary bomb:
We had to make a dash for it, not knowing that it was the start of the Manchester Blitz. I can vividly remember running down Clopton Street making for home. My brother grasped my hand and we tried to shelter in doorways from the falling shrapnel. The sky was on fire and we stood in the doorway of the Beehive pub, the Angel near the junction of Ward Street and Clopton Street, and dodged from doorway to doorway until we reached Mulberry Street library and ran downstairs to the shelter, which was full.

We ended up in the Hulme Town Hall shelter and settled down, with kiddies cuddling toys in the bunk beds of shelter, for thirteen hours non-stop bombing. We listened to the droning of the bombers; but we repeatedly sang *Begin the Beguine*. At 6 a.m. we emerged through an emergency exit on to the Stretford Road and I can see the devastation now. . . .

Now, thirty-eight years later, when I hear *Begin the Beguine* on the radio, I smile. I wonder if anyone else remembers that night of 'tropical splendour'—it sure was hot!

In the main cities all over the country people went to the public shelters every night. They took with them their dual-purpose inflatable capes which could be used to protect them from the rain during the day and as a temporary mattress at night. Others had a home-made shelter satchel, designed to carry a rug, which also had large pockets for books and knitting and smaller side pockets for sweets, cigarettes, playing cards, first-aid dressings and rubber ear plugs. Some people remained at home in their own, or their neighbour's, Anderson shelter in the garden or from March, 1941, in the new indoor Morrison shelter, a steel-topped table with wire mesh sides. But the majority of people didn't like shelters, either public or domestic. An official survey in London in November; 1940, showed that 60 per cent. of people did not use a shelter of any kind. Mrs J. Nessworthy, of South Shields, was one of these. 'My next-door neighbour had a little girl', she writes, 'and when the siren went we all used to dive under my dining room table. But the little girl would not go underneath unless the dog was also there, as it always howled if there was going to be a raid. We used to sing all the old songs to pass the time away'—and so did millions of other shelterers.

Mrs Jean Stokes, who was then living with her family near the docks in Sunderland, recalls that everyone in the shelter used to sing until the all-clear sounded. 'I think music helped to win the war', she writes. 'It gave us the courage to carry on.' Mrs O. Morgan, of Bristol, would agree. 'When the raids started', she says, 'my husband and I would sing to dare old Hitler. My husband would play the piano and off we went—*Roll Out the Barrel, (We're gonna hang out) The Washing on the Siegfried Line.*' When Mrs

Shelterers emerge to find devastation.
Overleaf: Collins's Music Hall,
Islington helped to keep up morale.

Hughes eventually reached home again after the first night of the Manchester blitz to find the rest of her family and the neighbours safe, they opened a small, precious bottle of whisky that they had been saving for Christmas, and got out her brother's gramophone and put on a record of Joe Loss playing *In the Mood*. 'We danced and laughed; it was great to be alive.' Over in Birmingham at about the same time Mr Ted Platt was playing another copy of the same record. 'During one of the first raids', he says, 'I took my second-hand portable gramophone down to the cellar and played and replayed the Joe Loss record of *In the Mood* with *Woodchoppers Ball* on the reverse. Even my father and my step-mother eventually adjusted to it.'

The blitz closed many places of entertainment in London—for a time. By 10 September 1940, only two theatres, the Criterion and the Windmill, were still open and soon there was only one which enabled the latter to make its proud boast of 'We never closed'. Variety theatres, including the Palladium and the Empires at Holborn, Finsbury Park, Stratford, New Cross and Penge were shut. Most cinemas remained open, but they were obliged to close at 9 p.m. Some dance halls never closed, including the Hammersmith Palais, but in many cities they had to shut early—at 9 p.m. in Stoke-on-Trent, for example. Pubs in the vulnerable areas of cities were also virtually deserted for a time.

A minority of people never gave up their evening's entertainment even during the worst air-raids, and they were soon joined by many others as the sight of enemy aircraft twisting and turning to escape the searchlights' beams, the wailing of sirens, the cracking of guns and the crunching of bombs became accepted hazards of the new night-time existence. Still bearing the scars of battle which they were to retain for the duration and for many years afterwards, the cities began to emerge cheerfully from their nightly ordeals. By 28 October 1940, a new matinée revue had opened at Wyndham Theatre in London and no one even moved when the sirens wailed. Variety theatres also re-opened. If there was an alert during the evening performance, as there usually was, the cast would invite the audience to stay on for an informal sing-song until there was a lull in the raid.

In compensation for their earlier closing hours, cinemas were allowed to open at 10.30 a.m., so that a few hours after the last bombs of the night had fallen on the capital a queue had started to form outside the Empire in Leicester Square to see that saga of another war, *Gone with the Wind*. This was by far the most popular and the longest-running film of the Second World War. Air-raids were announced by the cinema manager or by a notice on the screen; but very few people, who had often queued so long to get a seat, ever left. During raids, the circle was less popular with most people except for young lovers who found that their mutual entertainment was less likely to be disturbed by the prudish flashing of some middle-aged usherette's torch than it was in the back row of the stalls. Many cinemas were destroyed, usually by incendiary bombs, but there were remarkably few casualties. During the first blitz on Sheffield, for example, the Central Picture House was totally burnt out, but all 400 members of the audience

One of the famous series of
Guinness advertisements.

Another advertisement which
appeared in the *Illustrated London
News* in 1941.

escaped to safety. One cinema in Portsmouth was hit while it was showing a horror film starring Boris Karloff while another cinema in Birmingham which was showing *Gone with the Wind* also went—completely.

Pubs had been deserted in the evenings for a time, but they were soon packed again, even during raids. In 1941, Miss Hilda W. Davison, of Wolverhampton, was working at the county office of the Women's Land Army in Swynnerton, Staffordshire, and had lodgings in the Fitzherbert Arms opposite, which was then a simple village inn. At the beginning of the war, a large royal ordnance factory known locally as 'the dump' had been built on the outskirts of the village. She had been working late one night when she heard bombs falling, six in rapid succession followed by five more. 'I was rather shaken', she writes, 'and felt I would be happier, if no safer, in my lodgings, so I packed up and walked across to the Fitzherbert. I went in by the side door as usual, but the passage was packed with singing munition workers, and I had to force my way through. The whole pub was packed and positively rocked to the chorus of *She'll be Coming round the Mountain*, a popular song of the day. Safe in my own room upstairs, I was able to identify with the crowd below. I have never forgotten that night, and can still feel the "what the hell" atmosphere of those days.'

Dancers also remained undeterred by the blitz. In the *Melody Maker* for 23 November 1940, Mr S. Ramsden, of the Plaza Ballroom, Derby, was reported as saying: 'Business at the Plaza is marvellous. I am turning over 200 away

every Friday night. A few weeks ago I broke all records at a "certain town in the Midlands", where 1,120 danced and really enjoyed themselves whilst bombs were dropping all around.' Mr Ted Platt used to go right across Birmingham at least twice a week to visit his favourite dance hall. 'I was so keen on Saturday nights', he writes, 'that I would arrive at the dance hall about half-an-hour before dancing commenced. I used to watch Ted, the kindly old caretaker, light the emergency gas lights with a taper. Everyone carried on if the sirens went, and on particularly bad nights, the noise outside drowned the sound of the trio!' After one especially severe raid, it took him three hours to walk home right through the centre of the blazing city, with street after street filled with crunching glass and dazed people, who had been bombed out, wandering through the streets clutching bundles of clothes and suitcases. Musicians had some equally terrifying experiences on their way to and from work. Harry Parry, who was then leading a band at the Coconut Grove, fell into a bomb crater in the darkened streets one night. In an article in the *Melody Maker* in December, 1940, he described how he used to walk to work with 'the shrapnel coming down like hail, smacking down in the roadway from four miles up with such force as to cause great flashes of light like those from a tram jolting over the points.'

There were relatively few dance hall disasters. The worst occurred at the Café de Paris in Coventry Street, when thirty-four people were killed by a direct hit in March, 1941, including the bandleader Ken Johnson from Georgetown, in what is now Guyana, who was called 'Snakehips' for his skill in dancing. In the following month, Al Bowlly, the famous guitarist-vocalist who had sung with many of the big name bands and who is still thought by many people to have been the greatest singer of that age, was killed by a land-mine in his flat in London. Other musicians were injured. Arthur Young, for example, who was then leading his band on the Novachord at Hatchett's in Piccadilly, was hurt by a blast as he was entering the restaurant early in the blitz, but his injuries were not serious and he soon recovered.

No one could have predicted how Britain would take it. The Luftwaffe had first tried out its murderous technique on the defenceless city of Guernica during the Spanish Civil War; it had destroyed one-eighth of the city of Rotterdam on 14 May 1940, while surrender negotiations were in progress; and it had mounted its most sustained attack on the city of Warsaw in the first month of the war. But this was the first time in history that an uninvaded country had been subjected to such a ferocious and sustained bombardment from the air.

There was some panic, some selfishness, some looting. Those people who couldn't, or didn't, have to take it, flocked out of the cities every night or stayed away until the blitz was over. Profiteering landladies in safe areas offered to let two rooms for ten guineas a week for a three-month period.

It was a time of strange and fantastic rumours, just as it had been during the earlier invasion scare when everyone was talking about the thousand invasion barges which had only turned back because of heavy fog, and of the bodies of German soldiers washed up on the beaches, many of them charred by the defensive line of fire that the Royal Navy had lit in the English Channel. The rumours and the suspicions became even more bizarre during the blitz. In all parts of the country there were stories of flashing lights preceding raids and of bombers circling for hours while they waited for a signal from the ground. On 11 September 1940, the *Daily Herald* reported that a pack of Nazi playing cards had been found in a shelter somewhere in north London after a strange-looking man had panicked during a raid and suddenly vanished. In October, Charlie Kunz, the American pianist who had lived in Britain for twenty years, was falsely accused of sending coded messages to Germany by means of his piano playing during his broadcasts for the BBC. There were even some people who believed that the Germans had invented a bomb which could chase you round a corner!

In spite of all these rumours, morale remained extremely high and families and social classes were more united than they had ever been. Members of families who had not spoken to each other for years now pestered London councils for news of relatives. Social class became of much less importance as people shared their sufferings in the streets and commiserated with each other. Town halls were inundated with piles of clothing and blankets for the homeless. In every city, almost before the all-clear had sounded, emergency canteens staffed by volunteers and with only a row of packing cases for a counter, had appeared in the stricken streets to bring comfort and refreshment to blitz victims. In Sheffield, within twenty-four hours of the

Norwegian sailors who helped in the
Plymouth blitz.

first big blitz, the City Hall ballroom had been turned into an emergency restaurant with meals being brought in from field kitchens and from staff canteens. The Duke of Westminster offered many of his empty luxury flats in the West End to the LCC to house the homeless from the East End of London. When King George VI visited the East End to see the damage for himself, a man in the crowd shouted out 'You're a great king' and the king replied 'You're a great people.' This unparalleled unity of spirit still makes many older people believe that these grim years were the best and the greatest of their lives.

In Norwich, almost alone, there was some loss of morale after the sirens had sounded too late to prevent heavy casualties in one or two of the earlier raids on the city. But even there, many people became infected with the blitz spirit. When workmen arrived one morning to put a temporary roof on Mrs M. Holmes's house, they were astonished to find her young son playing *I'll be with you in Apple Blossom Time* on their damaged piano. In Plymouth, the citizens, the soldiers and the sailors danced defiantly on the Hoe after the city had been blitzed. There was a manic fury in much of the enjoyment. On 30 September 1940, the *Daily Mirror* had a headline: 'LET THE PEOPLE SING? YOU CAN'T STOP 'EM!' The picture below showed Cockneys dancing and singing in the devastated streets of the East End to the sounds of a harmonium perched precariously on the debris of their former homes. In one East End pub, the customers went on singing, even though their voices could scarcely be heard through the continual concussions of high explosives, while the landlord went round with a collecting box for the Spitfire Fund. When an underground shelter in a factory in south-west London was hit and the water main was shattered, the girls in one section sang *Roll out the Barrel* to their trapped workmates. Later in the war, a large part of the High Street in Exeter, including the Post Office, was destroyed in a raid on 3–4 May 1942. In a secret report, the Director-General of the GPO said: 'The telegraph staff who were on duty were working in the basement and when the building was destroyed

they were trapped; they interrupted the service for a few moments only to transmit particulars of their situation and of their next of kin, and then went on disposing of the traffic.' In the streets, the Union Jack fluttered proudly from the window of many a bombed home and blitzed shops displayed 'Business as Usual' signs on their sandbagged fronts. Other shops had notices saying 'If you think this is bad, you should see our Hamburg branch', while many pubs displayed signs saying 'Blast out—but not sold out.'

Mrs Eleanor Derbyshire of Cheetham, Manchester, still recollects the extraordinary cheerfulness and resolve of Mancunians at the start of the blitz. 'The blitz had been on all night and hell was loose. I was driving a mail van

A brief respite for a fireman in
Exeter, 1942.

ENSA entertains shelterers at
Aldwych Tube station, 1940.

and a postman who had been helping me with collections from the hospitals and mail boxes were returning when the all-clear sounded. Devastation was everywhere. At the corner of Gore Street and Greenheys Lane, Doctor Roy's surgery had been hit and he and two nurses had been killed. But this was war. Everybody had to *carry on*.

'We arrived at Radnor Street off Bradshaw Street. At the corner there was the Linwood Hotel. As there were not enough public shelters, the landlord had allowed the customers to shelter in the cellar until the all-clear sounded. They came out just as we were passing in the mail van. They saw the terrible devastation and they looked at us, who were very weary, and started singing *There'll always be an England*. That singing cheered us up, and we shouted back to them that there is always a tomorrow.'

> *There'll always be an England*
> *While there's a country lane*
> *Wherever there's a cottage small*
> *Beside a field of grain.*

The last big raid of the blitz and the biggest of the war on Britain came on 10 May 1941, when nearly 1,500 people were killed in London and another 1,800 were seriously injured. The Luftwaffe then transferred its attention to Russia, though there were still some other air-raids on Britain and later attacks by V1s and V2s. It was in one of these later air-raids that Mrs Ada Evans, of New Moston, was spending Saturday night in a shelter with her boy-friend who was on a forty-eight hour pass. 'We came out for a breath of fresh air and stood near a bridge overlooking the River Medlock in Beswick, Manchester. We could hear the sound of the guns not far away. We looked at each other and started singing *A Lovely Way to Spend an Evening*. Blackout and bombs could not dampen our spirits in those days; we were both eighteen and in love. I will always remember that episode. My boy-friend was killed in action nine months later.'

The National Savings Committee's
most famous character.

CHAPTER 5

IT'S FOOLISH BUT IT'S FUN

BY May, 1941, the war had already lasted twenty months, much longer than many people had expected and too long for others to endure unchanged. The early partings had already been extended into lengthy sightless separations for the wives of men who had been made prisoners of war or who had been posted out to the desert or to the Far East where an uneasy peace was still maintained until the Japanese attack on Pearl Harbour on 7 December 1941.

The wives of regular soldiers often had to endure the longest separations. 'My husband was a time-serving soldier in quite a famous regiment, the 17th–21st Lancers,' writes Mrs Helen P. Dickens of Corby, Northants, 'and had already been in India for a number of years. He had been back home in England for only a few weeks when he was recalled to the Far East again.' She still remembers their last night together when they went to the Blue Halls in Edinburgh, now demolished, and joined in the chorus of *A Nightingale Sang in Berkeley Square* with

tears streaming down their cheeks. On the way back to their billets, he sang *We'll Meet Again* to her. 'He served all through the Burma, South-East Asia and Japanese campaigns', she goes on. 'Our twin sons were five-and-a-half years old when he returned', though, as we shall see later, their reunion was not destined to last for many years.

For many other wives, lengthy separations from their husbands also started at this time when the Western Desert Force was being re-grouped into a greatly expanded Eighth Army. Mrs G. Farrell, of Stockport, Cheshire, always used to include the last verse of *Yours* in her letters to her husband.

Yours in the grey of December
Here or on far distant shores!
I've never loved anyone
The way I love you
How could I?
When I was born to be just Yours.

Mrs Farrell was just one of the many thousands of wives who lost their husband to the desert war and the

113

subsequent campaigns in Italy and Western Europe. 'I was married on 7 December 1940', she writes. 'My husband got a weekend pass to come home for the wedding. Six months later he went to the Middle East and I didn't see him again for four-and-a-half years.'

For many wives, particularly those with young children, the subsequent years were the most frustrating, the most depressing and the most lonely of their lives. Conscription had been introduced in December 1941 for single girls and childless widows between the ages of 20 and 30 and it was extended later to women between 18 and 51 years of age. Most of them were not conscripted into the women's Services, which usually had enough recruits, but they were directed into munition factories sometimes far away from home. Although wives were not forced to go out to work, many of them did so to make ends meet, travelling to work on crowded buses, queueing for offal and other off-ration foods, retrieving their young children from the home of a relative or a neighbour when they came home. Their nights were often spent in knitting, sewing and making do; cooking, bottling and writing letters to their absent husbands. Their only entertainment was listening to the radio or a rare visit to see a film or a friend. There were many 'door-step widows' of this kind. In a *Sunday Pictorial* anthology called *Sweethearts All*, published in 1945, one trooper, who had been captured by the Japanese in 1942, said that his wife had become 'almost a hermit, leaving the house only once a week to see a film'.

But for other women—the unattached, the detached, the young, the faithless, the older spinster whose faded looks were granted a new interest by any heavy concentration of troops—these years were the best of their lives, an endless round of fun and entertainment, of new dates and discoveries, of drinks and dances almost every night. The natural exuberance of youth would probably have made these teenage years exciting in any case, but the special circumstances of wartime, with their uniquely irresponsible atmosphere, still make them sparkle with unforgettable excitement in the memories of many women who are now in their fifties.

Money flowed freely for far more people than in pre-war days. Despite the propaganda of the National Savings Campaign, which spawned a fearsome, evil-looking character, the Squander Bug which everyone was urged to squash, many people continued to spend their money as they made it, or if they had been forced into involuntary savings by some extended period of active service at sea or in some remote theatre of war, they disbursed much of their accumulated wealth in one great round of bounty and extravagance. The only certain thing then was uncertainty itself, which helped to give the brief hours of leisure a quality of carefree immediacy. The soldier with whom you were dancing one night might be posted away the next day; the airman might never return from his mission; the sailor, unbeknown to himself, might be setting out on his last voyage. When all futures were so uncertain, everyone took more interest in the present hour, and they often related more easily and more genuinely to each other when consequences were difficult to foresee and when many of the rigid social barriers of pre-war days had been shattered. Although commissioned rank still perpetuated a social divide so that officers above the rank of major, squadron-leader or lieutenant commander rarely went to town-hall dances, commissions did not faithfully reflect either pre-war status or post-war potential, producing many anomalies in both the officer class and other ranks. At one extreme there were aristocrats serving as privates; and pre-war vacuum cleaner salesmen with commissioned rank. The whole of life on the home front was beginning to lose much of its pre-war starchy formalism, a change which was given a general welcome. 'The jovial conviviality of cosy, wartime receptions', wrote *Vogue* in April, 1942, 'is more appreciated than the rather impersonal bridal banquets of pre-war days.'

Dance halls were the great meeting place of wartime where men and women of varying social classes came together as they would never have done before the war. They provided a refuge from all the anxieties and frustrations of the dark outside world where couples could forget their cares for a while as they danced in each other's arms to bland tunes with their soft, comforting words. Many of the popular songs of the second half of 1941 were particularly romantic; *Let there be Love, You Stepped out of a Dream, You Started Something* and, of course, *Yours* which became one of the biggest hits of the war. Other songs such as *I've got Sixpence (As I go Rolling Home), I came, I saw, I conga'd*, and *I, Yi, Yi, Yi, Yi (I like you very much)* from the film *That Night in Rio*, starring Carmen Miranda with her floral head-dresses, added a touch of light-hearted jollity; while the entry of

Russia into the war after the German attack of 22 June 1941, produced a few songs with a Slav association, such as *Russian Rose*, which was the most popular; *My Katrina*, described by its publisher as a 'dynamic dance tune full of Russian flavour', and, later on, *Ya Vass Loublou (means 'I love you')*. Community dances from earlier years, such as the hokey-cokey, the conga and the palais glide became even more popular in the cheerful matey atmosphere of wartime dance halls, as did excuse-me-foxtrots. Quicksteps, which were more cheerful and lively, were preferred to waltzes, though the last waltz of all, with its promise of pleasures still to come, was always one of the most popular. *Goodnight Sweetheart*, which had retained its popularity from pre-war days, was often included in the final set of dances. It was followed by the last waltz, *Who's Taking you Home Tonight?* published in 1939, which was supplemented in 1942 by *The Anniversary Waltz*. 'You always knew who "fancied" you in those days', writes Mrs Iris Hutchings, of Knowle, Bristol. 'He made a bee-line for you, and if you fancied him too, well, war or no war, that made the perfect end to the evening.'

Most dance halls were crowded from the moment the doors opened until they closed. The girls wore dresses which had been dyed, braided or re-modelled to cover wartime austerity with new glamour, and the men wore uniforms of many different hues. There were also a few male civilians who often had a low priority among the dancing girls, and some servicewomen in uniform. From the first few months of the war servicewomen had been allowed to wear

Everyone takes the floor for the
Kangaroo Hop, 1941.

civilian clothes when they were off duty for more than twenty-four hours, but most of them did not avail themselves of the opportunity. The vast majority were volunteers and proud of their uniform. Mrs Iris Hutchings had been going to a very popular 'hop' for two years before the war where she had made many friends among the dancers and the members of the band. 'Then war broke out, and I joined the Land Army. Many of the dancers came to see me off as I set out in "me breeches, me hob nails and 'at" to change my life from dance shoes to "wellies". Fortunately, I wasn't sent too far away, so that I was able to get home every other weekend. So back I went to my old "haunt" dressed, of course, in my uniform which I was very proud to wear. Imagine my surprise when I entered the ballroom to the tune of *A Nightingale Sang in Berkeley Square* and the band

promptly switched to *I'm an Old Cowhand*. I was the "star" of the evening. This happened each time I went, and I must admit to feeling (at that time) that I was "somebody".'

Many of the girls, but fewer men, were expert dancers as the former discovered to their cost as their flimsy shoes were squashed by heavy army boots. Those who could dance well were much admired. The tango *Jealousy*, still revives powerful wartime memories for Miss Joan Stanhope of Fulford, York. 'They used to lower the lights and it was all rather sexy and daring compared with now', she writes. 'There was one rather curvy sort of girl who wore black patent leather shoes with crossed straps round the ankles. We christened her "Film Star Shoes", but she was a marvellous dancer. As she and her partner took the floor, there was a tense sort of atmosphere which that particular tune always revives for me. She usually wore a black dress and was disturbingly voluptuous.'

A former AC2 has different memories of the same tune. 'I was really taken', he writes, 'by a tall blonde who was always at the dance hall on Saturday nights. I'd asked her to dance once or twice, but she'd always refused. She was a marvellous dancer and I was so jealous when I saw her dancing to *Jealousy* in the arms of another airman that I decided to take some lessons. I came back all ready to display my skills, but she wasn't there that Saturday or the next. I made a few inquiries and found that she'd been called up and sent to a munitions factory 200 miles away!'

Couples who were particularly skilful at one kind of dance often danced together regularly. Miss Hilda May Whorton, of Wombourne, Staffs, who used to walk three miles along country lanes to attend a dance on Saturday night, writes: 'One airman, although accompanied by two girls, always danced the old-time waltz with me. One night they were in the refreshment room when the band struck up and he came out looking all round. I went up to him and asked if he was looking for me which, of course, he was. Shortly afterwards, he was posted to the Bahamas and that was the last I saw of him.'

Girls were never sure from one week to the next whom they would meet at dances, and this contributed to the sense of fun and excitement. As the strategic demands of war shifted whole regiments of troops from one base to another, the dance halls might be almost emptied of men so that girls were forced to dance with each other until the next great influx of troops. Despite the ceaseless warnings that 'Careless Talk Costs Lives', local people often knew when troops were going to move before some of the troops did themselves. These vast movements of allied troops gave many small towns an international character. Petersfield, in Hampshire, for example, was still a quiet country town in 1939, little visited by foreigners, but the huge army camps at Bordon and Longmoor and the naval base at Portsmouth transformed it into a great international resort which is still remembered by many Allied servicemen in all parts of the world. The streets and the ballroom in the Town Hall were made colourful with uniforms of many different hues: Polish sailors in their gaiters and baggy trousers; the berets and red pom poms of Free French sailors; the Canadians with their ornate shoulder flashes.

Other towns were similarly transformed. Many teenage girls made the rounds of all the nationalities, who soon acquired their separate and distinct reputations as experiences were subsequently recounted in bars and powder rooms, in offices and on the shop floor. One London housewife, who was a teenager at the beginning of the war, recalls how she and her friends reached the rather dogmatic conclusion that 'Englishmen were dull, honest and respectable, but incredibly unsophisticated. Canadians were crude, cheerful and often good dancers. Americans were wealthy, irresponsible and naïve. Their generosity was natural; but they were gullible enough to think that it guaranteed their popularity. The Poles were good-looking, untrustworthy and lecherous, with a great facility for learning English. The French sailors were good dancers, but there was a rumour that they were all criminals who had been released from gaol to join the Forces. They never bothered to learn to speak English.'

Before the war no respectable wives would have gone to dances without their husbands, but a few married women started to do so almost as soon as their husbands were posted out to the BEF and more and more wives, bored and lonely, joined them as the periods of separation lengthened into years. Some of them used to take off their wedding rings because they thought that men would not want to dance with married ladies! One schoolteacher from the West Country remembers how she stayed at home practically every night for six months after she was married in 1942 at the age of nineteen. 'I adored dancing,' she says, 'but my mother and an older woman in the office told me that it would be wrong for me to go to dances now that I was married. One hot summer night, I suddenly thought, "This is ridiculous." I went out that evening without telling my mother where I was going (I was still living with her then) and went to a dance. As I went in, the band was playing *The World is Waiting for the Sunrise*, which was a tune from the First World War, I think.* It sounded wonderfully enticing. I went into the ballroom, which was packed with soldiers and sailors, and after that it was sunshine all the way.'

Mrs Pat Gorner, of Southampton, was left alone with her baby son when her husband was posted overseas 'for six long years'. For part of that time she lived with another married woman with three

*It was actually published in 1920.

boys whose husband was also serving abroad. 'Next door was the fire station. There were two London firemen there and the four of us became friends. We did their mending and in return Harry would take Nellie out for a drink while George and I sat with the boys. The next night we would go out. By the way, I wrote and asked my husband if I could do this.'

There were thousands of uncomplicated wartime friendships of this kind which sometimes grew into stronger attachments. Mrs Peggy Smith, of Wolverhampton, who lived in Surrey during the war, writes: 'I was married but separated from my husband and had two children. I was very frightened and most unhappy, but a woman friend persuaded me to go to a local dance, where I met a Canadian soldier. We danced and talked and became friends. From being a person who didn't even want to live (my husband had written to say he loved someone else), I found some happiness, though only for a short time, as those Canadian boys were sent to Italy. The man I met who was so good and kind to me was killed.'

Most girls went to dance halls to dance, to have fun and for comradeship; but as many lonely Servicemen had different ideas and demands, practically all girls were forced into compromising situations from time to time. In spite of the long periods of separation, most married women were surprisingly faithful to their absent husbands in those pill-less days when sex was still an ultimate favour granted only to the loved or the extremely persistent—checkmate and not an opening gambit. The long years of separation, however, when women learnt to cope without their husband, contributed towards their emancipation,

A dramatic official poster. Overleaf:
The Free French pub in Soho, 1941.

giving them a new feeedom and independence. Although sex was not discussed as openly or intelligently as it is now, there was an increasingly frank and mature attitude towards it, which was reflected in the agony columns of women's magazines. In January, 1942, Mrs F wrote to *Everywoman*: 'I took a war job in a factory while my husband was in the Army. When he went out East I felt the world had come to an end, I was so lonely. Then I met a man at a dance. I'm not excusing myself, but I drifted until I became unfaithful to my husband. Now I'm horrified. I've given up the man —but what shall I say to my husband? I'm not really an unfaithful type of woman at all!'

Before the war such a letter would almost certainly have resulted in stern homilies, but the answer was full of sympathy: 'Do get that guilty feeling out of your mind or you will destroy every chance of future happiness for yourself and your husband. What happened is a direct result of the war—you were thrown out of your circle and into a new environment. . . . Don't say a word to your husband. Silence is the bravest thing.' As Victorian prudery began to vanish, people started to treat sex more naturally and even to laugh about it. The first and only issue of a typewritten magazine published by an ARP post, Newnham Croft Depot, Cambridge, suggested that the 'armorial bearings of the depot should contain the figures of: two female ambulance drivers dormant, two first aiders couchant, surmounted by one caretaker rampant'.

The Paramount Salon de Danse, Tottenham Court Road, 1941.

It was not easy for women to look their best in wartime though by the use of ingenuity, skill and, occasionally, the black market many of them contrived to look quite presentable. Clothes rationing had started on 1 June 1941, with sixty-six coupons for the year which had been reduced to forty by the end of the war, though the unscrupulous could always buy coupons on the black market for a shilling or two each. The Board of Trade supported rationing with a massive advertising campaign. One of their advertisements under the headline 'PATRIOTIC PATCHES' started: 'A neatly patched garment is something to be proud of nowadays. To discard clothes that are not completely worn out is as unpatriotic as to waste good food.' But the appeal to patriotism was unnecessary as clothes rationing was accepted in the same spirit as the rationing of food as one of the unfortunate necessities of war, which was preferable to a free-for-all which could only benefit the wealthy. In fact, the spirit of democratic levelling had by then been so generally accepted that as *Vogue* observed in January, 1942, it looked wrong to look wealthy. 'Glance round a smart restaurant any evening and what strikes the eye as right? The simple dinner dresses, the simple day dresses, the simple suits. . . .'

By January, 1942, the first Utility clothes, which were cheap and simple but well cut, had appeared in the shops: Dereta offered a New Era coat for eighty-three shillings and elevenpence. The two-piece suit in hard-wearing tweed, which could be given a new look each day through different blouses and accessories, was so popular that by the middle of 1942 it had become, according to *Vogue*, 'almost a civilian uniform'. Dresses, which just covered the knees, were simple, straight and often dark in colour, black being preferred for dances. Pinafore dresses, dirndl skirts and sweaters with dolman sleeves were all popular.

There had never been so much knitting, not only of 'comforts' for the troops but also of women's clothes, including Victory sweaters with V necks and a V motif in the pattern, cardigan suits, and long woollen stockings. Silk stockings, which cost from three shillings and elevenpence to one guinea a pair, had disappeared by the early months of 1941, though old ones could still be repaired for sixpence a ladder and threepence for each adjacent one. Artificial silk stockings were still produced, but as they became scarce, many girls started to go without, particularly in the summer, using leg make-up or sun-tan lotion to give the appearance of stockings, with a seam added by an eyebrow pencil. Slacks, which became acceptable wear for women during the war, were even more popular in winter, though there were still some conservative employers who refused to let girls wear them to work. Shoes, which also became increasingly scarce, were often wedge-heeled with peep toes.

Women's magazines tried to rival the official 'Mrs Sew and Sew' by producing ingenious ideas for making old clothes look new and attractive. Surplus army blankets could be dyed and made into capes. Fringe and braid, which were off the ration like buttons and ribbons, could be used in a variety of ways. Cartridge-pleated ribbons were stitched on to old blouses and dresses; new braided lapels were added to old suits;

Recommended Ministry of Labour
hairstyles for safety in factories.

dance shoes were refurbished with old pieces of brocade stitched on with curved surgical needles which could still be bought at one shilling and sixpence for a packet of six. There was even greater ingenuity with clothes which did not show. Army surplus pants, which cost four shillings a pair, could be cut down to make warm winter knickers; old brassieres could be starched to prolong their life, though not without some discomfort to the wearer; cami-knickers could be made from heavy, rustling parachute silk. In 1940, *Miss Modern* showed its readers how to make five smart hats from a yard of felt; but later in the war many women started to dispense with hats altogether or to wear a headscarf or a turban.

Hair styles have rarely been more ugly than they were in wartime. One of the most popular, the Victory roll, had a huge roll of hair on the top of the head and often a large soft wave behind it, while the rest of the hair was scraped back behind the ears with the ends dropping lankly on to the shoulders. The Even Steven was somewhat more elegant with a middle parting and tight curls at the back and sides. Many girls copied the hair style of Veronica Lake, who had created a sensation with her appearance as a torch singer in the film *I Wanted Wings* with her hair dangling long and loosely over one cheek. The page-boy style in which the hair was curled under at the ends was also very popular and rather nice.

Cosmetics became increasingly scarce, though they could still be obtained from 'spivs' or 'wide boys' who wore camel hair coats with padded shoulders or Zoot suits with a chain dangling down one leg. One popular song of 1941–2 was *A Zoot Suit (For my Sunday Girl)*. By January, 1942, the supplies of all reputable cosmetics had been reduced to one-quarter of the pre-war level and in February of that year, soap went on ration for the first time. The women's magazines produced some equally ingenious suggestions for looking

Everyone was a friend in wartime.

beautiful without cosmetics. Beetroot juice was recommended as a replacement for lipstick; powdered orris root could be used for a dry shampoo; vaseline could replace eye shadow; an infusion of camomile leaves could take the place of a golden rinse; and the nail buffer could be brought out again if no nail varnish was obtainable. In spite of *ersatz* substitutes and Utility clothes, girls still seemed beautiful in the eyes of thousands of lonely boys who were miles away from home.

CHAPTER 6

MA, I MISS YOUR APPLE PIE

NO other allies had such a profound impact on wartime Britain as the Americans. The first GIs arrived on 26 January 1942, when two troop transports carrying nearly 3,000 men reached Belfast. As the tide of GIs spread across the countryside from air bases in East Anglia to army camps in the West Country, life on the home front was affected in many ways, both great and small. The dance hall scene altered considerably at this time as the GI presence and the growing fondness for things American made jazz, swing music and jitterbugging increasingly popular.

An interest in jazz, which had started as a minority cult among English musicians and students in the Twenties, had been encouraged in the inter-war years by the formation of many Rhythm Clubs, sponsored by *Melody Maker*, the first being formed in London in June, 1933. Louis Armstrong had played in London in 1932, Duke Ellington in 1933 and Cab Calloway in the following year when, under union pressure from both sides of the Atlantic, jazz bands and

dance orchestras were banned from playing in each other's country in a misguided attempt to decrease unemployment among musicians. After 1934, jazz fans had to rely on records, short-wave broadcasts and the native efforts of such groups as George Chisholm and his Jive Five. The first British jazz jamboree was held in March, 1939, at the Gaumont State, Kilburn and the second in the same place a year later. Although both jamborees were sell-outs, they included some bands which true fans would scarcely have associated with jazz, such as van Dam and his Orchestra, George Melachrino and Maurice Winnick! The BBC's Radio Rhythm Club, which was first broadcast in 1939, did more to encourage an interest in true jazz: the resident sextet, led by the clarinettist, Harry Parry, featured the blind pianist George Shearing.

Swing music, another importation from the United States, was no novelty in Britain in 1942, but it became increasingly popular as the war went on. The swing era had started in 1935 when

Benny Goodman formed a band using Fletcher Henderson arrangements to play at the Palomar Ballroom in Los Angeles; his sweet renderings of popular songs and jazz classics, skilfully arranged to display the individual abilities of star soloists, was an instantaneous success. Many American band leaders, including Artie Shaw, Tommy Dorsey and Charlie Barnet, got in the same groove, and there were numerous British imitators. Wartime ballrooms swung to such tunes as *In the Mood, Tuxedo Junction*, and *American Patrol* all made famous by Glenn Miller; *Woodchoppers Ball* and *Caldonia* which were always associated with Woody Herman; and *Night and Day* which was linked with Artie Shaw. The arrival of the GIs helped to give the sounds of 1942 an even more indigenous American flavour with such songs as *Ma, I Miss Your Apple Pie, Chattanooga Choo Choo, Deep in the Heart of Texas* and *Praise the Lord and Pass the Ammunition*—a phrase which had first been used by an American chaplain to encourage men during the Japanese attack on Pearl Harbour.

For many years, enthusiasts had been accustomed to tuning in late at night on their powerful, super-heterodyne, short-wave receivers to hear the latest American swing records before they were on sale in Britain. From July, 1943, some British people could hear them more easily on the American Forces Network, though as its low-powered transmitters in Britain were beamed towards the main American bases, it was only people in the vicinity who could hear the broadcasts

The American Army Air Force Swing Sextet playing in the Eagle Club, London.

clearly. Mr Ralph Jeffrey, of Sale, Cheshire, was more fortunate. At one time during the war, when he was practising receiving Morse signals at speed, the instructor played the American Forces Network in the background 'as "interference" and for his own pleasure. Every day at 11 a.m. he tuned into *Duffle Bag*, introduced by PFC "Muff it" Moffat, and each day for weeks—four or five, I think—Moffat played his own particular favourite, *I'll Walk Alone* sung by Lily Anne Carroll. My Morse suffered, but I was word perfect on the song!'

The GIs brought American bands to Britain once again. There had long been a number of Americans leading British dance bands—Carroll Gibbons, Roy Fox, Jack Harris—but these bands were something different, the greatest luminaries of American show business. In June, 1944, Artie Shaw's US Navy Band made a tour of American camps, though it was led by Sam Donohue as Artie Shaw had just been discharged from the US Navy on medical grounds. The arrival of Glenn Miller in the following month created even greater excitement as his unique style of playing had made his music the most popular wartime sound with both Americans and Britons. Almost nothing else can bring back such strong memories of those crowded wartime dance halls than the tunes for which he became famous: his signature tune, *Moonlight Serenade, In the Mood* and *Little Brown Jug*. Glenn Miller fans, of whom there are still a considerable number, continue to argue about his greatest achievements. 'Most of the Miller fans I knew in the Forties', writes Mr Ralph Jeffrey, 'preferred *Falling*

Leaves and *A String of Pearls* to *Little Brown Jug*, but the film created a legend.'

Glenn Miller and his forty-six piece AAF band gave seventy-one concerts for the American forces and made innumerable broadcasts and recordings during their six months' stay in Britain. There were few opportunities for Britons to see the band live. One of those rare occasions came on 27 July 1944, when they played on the stage at the Plaza Cinema in London before the screening of a Bing Crosby film. On 14 December 1944, Glenn Miller, who had never liked flying, set off in an American general's plane, for Paris to entertain the GIs in France, but his plane crashed on the way. The news that Glenn Miller was missing was just as profound a shock to his millions of fans as any major defeat or disaster of the war. He had become such a legend in his lifetime that some people were reluctant to accept the true facts of his death and rumours quickly started to spread which still gain some false credence to this day. It was said that his plane had been shot down by the Germans, that Miller had arrived in France only to be killed in a brothel brawl, that his fellow-passenger, a colonel, was involved in the black market and had shot Miller and the pilot before he landed the plane himself safely in France. All of the stories were false.

Another false assumption, which is still repeated constantly, is that jitterbugging did not start in Britain until the arrival of the GIs. But, even before the war began, smart young things, who had caught the fever in the United States, were jitterbugging in basement rooms of London night clubs and by 1940 the craze had spread so widely that many ballrooms, particularly in the Midlands, had been forced to ban it to avoid inconvenience to other dancers and damage to their precious sprung floors. The MC at one Midlands ballroom—the Palace, Erdington, Birmingham—allowed the fever of one small group of enthusiasts to burn itself out in a solo demonstration every Saturday night. 'By Easter, 1940', Mr Ted Platt writes, 'my

with complete respect for the orthodox steps of English ballroom dancing. If any of us were missing from the floor at jitterbug time on Saturday night, our names were called out over the microphone—to a great round of applause!' By that time, too, the first national jitterbug championship had been held at the Paramount in London and in February, 1940, after a jitterbug

The Mecca Ballroom at Covent Garden.

little crowd of friends, about eight of both sexes, had definitely got the bug. We had the whole floor to ourselves, with the other dancers standing round the sides, gazing intently at what must have seemed to them like *Saturday Night Fever* as it appears to our generation today!

'The band always played *My Heart Belongs to Daddy* which gives plenty of scope for the drummer to quicken the beat. After ten to fifteen minutes we were cured for that night, and, sweating profusely, we were then content to dance

jamboree at Mac's Club in Great Windmill Street, London, a new Federation of Rug Cutters and Swing Cats had been formed!

Jitterbugging, which was only suitable for the young, the fit and the uninhibited, quickened the whole tempo of the dance hall. Even Victor Silvester formed a separate jive band in 1943, though his Ballroom Orchestra with its strict tempo beat formed in 1934 and his BBC Dancing Club programme, first broadcast in 1941, continued to be extremely popular with traditional dancers. Jitterbugging took dancing back to its primitive origins of exuberant self-expression within a prescribed ritual. A similar change had occurred towards the end of the First World War when society girls in long black stockings, short boots and peg-topped skirts had danced the bunny hug and the turkey trot in counterpoint to the booming guns of the mindless slaughter in the trenches.

The arrival of the GIs transformed what had been a minority cult into a general fashion so that it was no longer the skilful tangoists who attracted envious glances but the jitterbugging GI and his English girl friend who were accorded their own respected territory, protected by a circle of admiring spectators. One former petty officer who was very keen on dancing, returned to Britain in 1942 after having been abroad for nearly three years. He says: 'I shall always remember the night I went back to my favourite ballroom at home. Everything was changed. The beat of the music was faster and firmer and instead of a graceful, horizontal circling of people round the floor, the heads of all the dancers were bobbing up and down.' In dance halls all over the country, the notices banning jitterbugging were removed or ignored as hep cats and hot hoses pecked, trucked and did the shag step. Legs clad in nylons, the gift of a friendly partner, went shooting out and skirts flew up revealing all, when only a couple of years before some girls had still been using modesty clips to hold their skirts down while they were cycling. The chains of modesty and prudence, which had bound so many women were weakened even more.

Many young women and teenage girls were completely captivated by the Americans. Mrs Alice Solomon, of Brandon, near Durham, who is still 'old-song mad', lived on the outskirts of London during the war. She loved singing and dancing and remembers how 'we used to struggle through the blacked-out streets and sing and dance with the American GIs. The Yankees loved us English girls and used to spend £10 on us with jewellery, gifts, dancing and nights out on the river in boats.' There are many other women in their fifties who still treasure memories of those happy carefree years of their youth. For Mrs Sheila Roberts, of Costessey, Norwich, the song *I'll be Seeing You* still brings back memories of her first meeting with a young American boy towards the end of the war, when she was fifteen and 'so much in love, even though I knew at the back of my mind that it could not last.' Her parents used to invite British and American servicemen to their home most weekends for a meal, a sing-song and a dance in the living room. Among them was one fair-haired American who was 'her ideal'. One Christmas, the British boys invited her to a concert and a dance which was being held in a village hall about five miles away. At 10.30 p.m., knowing that she had a long walk home through country lanes, she was just about to leave when the band started playing her favourite tune, *I'll be Seeing You*, her party piece which she used to sing and play on the piano.

'I guess you know what happened next', she writes. 'A quiet American voice said, "Honey, would you please dance with me?" Yes, it was the young American whom I had always adored.

A British tribute to the Stars and
Stripes at a Hallowe'en party.

Knowing that I liked the song, he had asked the band leader to play it. I found out later that he had asked my parents where I was, and asked permission to meet me, to walk me home, and to take me out on dates in the future. By then I was sweet sixteen. Each date we had, he always asked my parents first.' Another event impressed the song even more firmly on her memory. 'The great Glenn Miller came to his station at Attlebridge to celebrate the station's 100 missions. The icing on the cake for us was that the orchestra played our tune. I danced the soles off my shoes that night. Even though I had no clothing coupons left, it was worth it.'

There were many genuine friendships and romantic encounters of this kind, but the GIs also attracted the attentions of other kinds of girls which shocked both many Britons and more sensitive Americans. The area around Rainbow Corner near Piccadilly Circus became notorious for its hordes of prostitutes, many of them part-time, flashing the beams of their masked torches on to their gold-chained ankles in the black-out. Robert S. Arbib Jr, an American sergeant stationed in East Anglia, was equally appalled by the free-and-easy behaviour of some girls in Ipswich who walked along the street at nights in pairs, wearing tight sweaters, short skirts and flat-heeled shoes, whispering 'Hi, Yank' to every passing GI. They filled the pubs to overflowing and crowded out the dance halls. At 10 p.m. when the pubs closed there was singing, laughing, shouting, scuffling and

US soldiers at Rainbow Corner.
Overleaf: The Allies toast each other
with English beer.

fighting in the streets, with couples petting in some doorways and urine running down into the gutter from others. An hour later, the trucks would arrive to take the GIs back to camp, attended by American military policemen with their white helmets, gloves and gaiters, appropriately nick-named 'Snowballs' by the English girls.

The genuine charm of many GIs, however, melted many British hearts. Their open-handed generosity, their easy friendliness, their effortless affluence seemed then to substantiate all the images of the great American dream which had been so carefully nurtured and disseminated by Hollywood in the years between the wars. By British standards, the Americans were rich, oh so rich, even if Britain had not already been further impoverished by more than two years of total war. The PX was a vast cornucopia of long-vanished delights to those who had second-hand access to it through the generosity of any GI, whose stores were so illimitable that they could apparently be showered also on to friendly allies. No GI was safe from the friendly importuning of young boys and girls, who ran after them in the street calling out 'Any gum, chum?' or 'Any candy, Andy?' Cigarettes were so cheap in the PX, only threepence for twenty, that no GI bought them by the packet but by the carton of ten, a striking display of affluence to British eyes then. Cartons of *Lucky Strike* and *Camel* cigarettes found their way into many British homes with bars of delicately-scented soap, which had gone on the ration a month after the first GIs arrived, razor blades of pre-war quality, and those precious nylons that no British girl had ever seen before. British air crews were delighted to be diverted in fog to some American air base in East Anglia, from which they would eventually return regaled with such unobtainable delicacies as chicken and ice-cream, which was no longer made in Britain after September, 1942.

There were many other goods which came into British homes—huge tins of corned beef, cookies, dried apples, prunes. Some of the attraction was based upon the greed of a poor, rationed and war-weary nation, which soured into envy among many British servicemen who resented their allies' greater affluence. An American private earned as much as a British Army captain. With their American billfolds stuffed fat with English pound notes, the GIs could get the best of everything: the best rooms in hotels, practically all the taxis, and, so it seemed then, the most attractive and the most nubile girls.

The comforting reassurance of having such an immensely rich and powerful ally, however, helped to conquer much of the residual opposition to the American way of life. Mr Stan White, of Kettering, Northants, remembers that as an eleven-year-old schoolboy he had a woman music teacher who had a great liking for traditional songs such as *Billy Boy* and *Dashing Away with the Smoothing Iron*. One day a friend of his started to sing *Mairzy Doats and Dozy Doats* in class. The teacher was furious with him for singing such 'rubbish', which she equated with the deplorable American habit of chewing gum. But they all got a shock, a very pleasant one for them, when shortly afterwards they began to practise for the annual carnival to raise money for

Kettering General Hospital. 'Imagine our surprise when she announced that we would be singing *Thanks, Mr Roosevelt* when we marched in the procession. It seemed fantastic at the time to hear this being rehearsed in the school hall. Soon all the classes were busy making crêpe paper dresses and Uncle Sam hats and a big banner bearing the title of the song. I did not take part, but I remember watching the kids go by, all dressed up in American colours and singing that song'.

What a mouthful! A Christmas party
for US airmen, 1942.

CHAPTER 7

LILLI MARLENE

POPULAR songs were an important element in the ceaseless battle of words which raged throughout the Second World War. Radio stations vied with each other to attract the greatest number of listeners among enemy troops by employing girl announcers with the softest and the most seductive voices to introduce programmes which included more music than talk. The BBC had considerable success with its broadcasts to the Germans by providing an alternative in the early years of the war to the endless round of marching and propaganda songs with which the Nazi dictators sought to sustain the morale of the German nation. Despite the inherent German predilection for martial songs and the Nazi ban on listening to foreign broadcasts, Jack Payne's programme *Moods Modernistic* went down well with many Germans, and as late as 1941 some German fans managed to let the BBC know by circuitous means that they would like to hear more. Another programme at this time was specially designed for the

Luftwaffe and featured many RAF dance bands. One of the most successful programmes, broadcast in the German-language service, was *Aus der Freien Welt*, a fifteen-minute session of jazz and swing, the kind of 'decadent, non-Aryan' music that the Nazi dictators had totally banned, but which some Germans, nevertheless, liked to hear. The popularity of these programmes with both German troops and civilians forced Goebbels to start a Forces Programme in 1942, two years after the BBC.

The enemy employed similar techniques. In the Far East, Enemy Anne, whose real name was Iva Toguri, used to introduce her Radio Tokyo broadcasts to Allied Servicemen with the words: 'This is your little playmate Enemy Anne, calling all of you orphans in the Pacific.' Thousands of veterans of the Anzio landings in Italy still remember 'husky-voiced Helen', the star of the German programme, *Jerry's Front*. Leaflets dropped on Allied troops advertised her broadcasts from 2 a.m. to 3 a.m. as 'the night bird's show with

Lale Andersen (Lilli Marlene)
thumbs a lift at the end of the war.

lovely (it's a pity you can't see her) husky-voiced Helen conducting the proceedings. You boys who suffer from insomnia will feel better disposed towards the German gunners who keep you awake.' Another programme from 10.30 p.m. to 11 p.m. was described as 'a snappy half-hour of dance tunes with a few news items and practically NO TALK!'

Propaganda, consisting of as few words as possible, was carried in on the wings of popular song whose sentiments were often twisted by parody or irony to deepen their appeal. *Home Town*, a song made famous by Flanagan and Allen in 1937, was played at the start of German broadcasts giving details of British casualties and prisoners-of-war. (It was also the title of a BBC record request programme to Malta compered by the Cockney actor Ronnie Shiner.)

J'Attendrai, which was published in May, 1939, and which retained its popularity with both the British and the French for the duration, was also used in the war of words. The French section of the BBC used a parody of it to assure their compatriots that victory would re-unite the whole nation one day, both those in occupied France and the Free French in Britain.

Other songs, with a simple, but virtually indefinable, appeal sped across all frontiers. The outstanding song of this kind was, of course, *Lilli Marlene*, (*Lili Marleen* in German) which was sung with equal fervour by soldiers in the Afrika Korps and in the Eighth Army; by Germans marching Yugoslav hostages to their death and by opposing partisans; by Sicilian peasants in the fields and by the invading Canadian soldiers; and by civilians in Germany and in the occupied

141

countries where millions of cheap copies were published by the Germans in many languages.

You wait where that lantern softly gleams,
Your sweet face seems to haunt my
*   dreams*
My Lilli of the lamplight,
My own Lilli Marlene.

The song had curious origins. The lyric was originally written as a poem during the First World War by Hans Leip, a poet and novelist, who was born in Hamburg in 1893. Mr Oswald Edwards, ALCM, of Ruthin, Clwyd, who served as a lance-corporal with 239 Company, RFC, from the Sicily landings to the final defeat of Germany, met Leip, 'a most charming gentleman' in his 'lovely home in Blankenese', a suburb of Hamburg, at the end of the last war. Leip, who was a guards fusilier in the First World War, told him that he wrote the poem on the eve of a battle on the Russian front in 1915. It was included in a slim volume of Leip's poems, *Die Hafenorgel*, which was published in 1937. 'The sentimental appeal of the words', says Mr Edwards, 'had much to do with its great popularity'. The poem was set to music in 1938 by Norbert Schultze, who was born in Brunswick in 1911. A composer of operettas, ballets and film music, he also wrote a very different kind of wartime song, *Bombs on England*, as well as *Lilli Marlene*. 'The tune itself is musically very commonplace', says Mr Edwards, 'and that no doubt was responsible for the high popularity it enjoyed during the war among armies on both sides—German and Italian, British and all the armies of the Allied Forces.'

Lilli Marlene was recorded in German just before the war by Lale Andersen, the daughter of a Bremerhaven sailor, who died in Vienna in 1972 at the age of fifty-nine. It was not a great success until it was broadcast in the middle of 1941 from the German Forces radio station in Belgrade to members of the Afrika Korps. These transmissions were also heard by British troops and *Lilli Marlene* eventually became the song of the whole desert. The Germans were quick to seize on its propaganda value and constructed loudspeaker units on lorries with a short range of about 200 yards to relay it to members of the Eighth Army. More sophisticated equipment was used later by both sides for propaganda purposes during the Italian landings and the Normandy invasion and by the end of the war the Americans had powerful loudspeakers on tank mounts with a range of about two miles.

Thousands of Eighth Army veterans still remember how they were treated to a free nightly rendering of the song by the Germans. Mr Albert McGrath, of Avonmouth, Bristol, says he will always recall that cold, clear night in the Western Desert in 1942 when he heard it being sung in German through the huge loudspeakers which 'Jerry' had mounted on the backs of lorries safely within their own lines. 'I liked it from the start, though others didn't; but I can assure you that everyone around me listened, and especially when it was later sung in English. Those who returned from the next day's fierce tank battle didn't exactly go for it the next night; but its captivating melody has held me right up till now, thirty-six years later, though I never forget, as well, the headstones I was to see at El Alamein War Cemetery of many who must have joined in "Underneath the lantern. . . ."' Mr John Trickett, of Edinburgh, who was a teenager during the war, also liked it for a very different reason. 'It was the first, and only, song I ever learned off by heart', he writes, 'and having had a stammer all my life, it gave me a great deal of pleasure.'

Fearing that the great popularity of *Lilli Marlene* might demoralise the troops, Whitehall commissioned a well-known song writer, Tommie Connor, who had had a hand in many successes, including the *Chestnut Tree* and *The Biggest Aspidistra in the World*, to write an English version. It was published in 1944 and was recorded by Anne Shelton in Britain and by Marlene Dietrich in the United States. But the concern about morale was unnecessary. Long before Tommie Connor had written his words, the troops had composed their own versions in both bawdy and respectable forms. Mr Edwards writes that the Eighth Army version started:

There was a song that the Eighth Army used to hear,
In the lonely desert, lovely, sweet and clear.
Over the ether came the strain, the soft refrain each night again
With you–Lily Marlene, with you–Lily Marlene.

After Rommel's defeat, they added another verse:

Afrika Korps has vanished from the earth,
Smashed soon the swine that gave it birth;
No more we'll hear that lilting strain, that soft refrain, each night again,
With you–Lily Marlene, with you–Lily Marlene.

Many parodies of songs were written during the war to add a cruel twist to the original words or to mollify the impact of unwelcome emotion. Thousands of original compositions were also written by both professional and amateur musicians in the Forces. Song-writing had been one of the most popular hobbies before the war when thousands of optimistic amateurs had sat down at their pianos every day to compose the masterpiece which they hoped might transform them into Irving Berlins overnight. Music publishers' offices in Denmark Street were bombarded daily with their fledgling efforts, for riches could be amassed by successful song-writers in those days before pop groups started to compose their own music and lyrics. Sheet music could have enormous sales in those pre-war days when many more people than now played the piano, the piano-accordion, the mouth organ, or the ukelele—if they were aspiring George Formbys. *Melody Maker* used to publish reviews of amateur efforts by 'Swinger' who could often be caustic in his comments. In November, 1939, he wrote:

I Love you So: Lyric—just tripe. Music—just hack work, if properly rewritten.
A Quiet Little Corner with Lora: The first line of your lyric looks ridiculous, 'Lora, a quiet little corner with you.' By the way, you write 'quite' for what is evidently meant to be 'quiet'—and I fancy you meant the girl's name to be 'Lorna' to rhyme with 'corner'. Anyway, this lyric has no guts to it. Not a patch on the conductor's lyric you submitted last month.

During the war with its need for

One of HMS Wolverine's crew
playing his mandolin on a gun
platform.

impromptu concerts to while away the boring hours between bouts of intense activity on land, on sea and in the air, the amateurs had a field day. Even children joined in. Mrs Tyszkiewicz, who was evacuated to a place 'somewhere in Wales', remembers how she and her friends used to sing their own version of *Roll out the Barrel*, which went:

Roll out the Army,
Roll out the Navy as well,
Roll out the Air Force
We'll bomb old Hitler to hell.
Now's the time to roll out the Forces
In a real air raid.

Mr Stan White, who watched the *Thanks, Mr Roosevelt* procession in Kettering, also recalls a couple of parodies of popular songs that wartime children used to sing. One of them, to the tune of *The Chestnut Tree*, whose original words had been written by Tommie Connor, went:

Underneath the spreading chestnut tree,
Neville Chamberlain said to me,
If you want to get your gas mask free
Join the blinking ARP.

The song expressed the resentment early in the war of officious wardens which only disappeared after they had proved their worth in the Blitz; but the words were inaccurate. Although wardens were issued with a more elaborate military-style gas mask, all civilians got theirs free of charge with gas helmets for babies with a concertina-type air pump operated by the mother; 'Mickey Mouse' gas masks for children up to five years of age which had two round eye-pieces and which were gaily painted in red and blue to make them more attractive; and the normal gas masks for adults and other children with a single eyepiece.

The other song that Mr White remembers was sung to the tune of *Whistle while you Work* from Walt Disney's film *Snow White and the Seven Dwarfs*. It went:

You whistle while you work,
Mussolini bought a shirt,
Hitler wore it–Musso tore it,
You whistle while you work.

Some children sang another version:

Whistle while you work,
Hitler is a twerp,
He's half barmy
And his Army,
So whistle while you work.

Resentment of the cigarette shortage produced a parody of *You are my Sunshine*:

You are my sunshine,
My double Woodbine
My box of matches
My Craven A.

The original version ran:

The other night dear, as I lay dreaming,
I dreamt that you were by my side,
Came disillusion when I awoke dear
You were gone, and then I cried—
You are my sunshine,
My only sunshine,
You make me happy,
When skies are grey.

Some of the adult efforts were far more creditable, particularly in the field of bawdy songs such as *The Ball of Kerriemuir*, which might be described as the wartime classic, and *Mersa Matruh* and *Ivan Skavinsky Skavaar*. The composers' identities remains one of the great unsolved mysteries of the war; some of them were attributed by widespread rumour then to well-known professionals in the entertainment world. Many of the original songs and parodies sung by soldiers, sailors and airmen at their impromptu concerts in all parts of the world expressed a love-hate relationship with the service they could not avoid.

Mr W. A. Jones, of Brentry, Bristol, served in an AMC for the first three years of the war. He used to do the first act in the concert party, with a friend who played the guitar, and he still has some notes, scribbled on a naval message pad at sea, of the songs they sang, which included: *Daisy, Beer, Glorious Beer, I Belong to Glasgow, All of Me, One Night of Love, I joined the Navy, It's a sin to tell a Lie, The greatest mistake of my life*. They also sang their own words to a medley of popular songs. One of them ran:

Now, I'm just an old crow,
By that you can guess
By the look in my eyes
And the way that I dress.
Now I get 10A every time I come out,
When the jaunty sees me, he always sings out
Oh, you were meant for me,
And I was meant for you.
You've got 10A and when you have done
We'll use you for a swabber to swab out the
  gun.
Because I yi yi yi yi yi yi like you werry
  mutch
I yi yi yi yi yi yi think you're grand
Get your hands around that holystone
And go and get a ton or two of sand.
Oh, you don't have to tell me I know
That look in your eyes tells me so
And I know off by heart

All the routine, sweetheart,
That if I'm adrift,
In the cells I will go,
For make and mend don't worry me
I'm under punishment, can't you see?
And they gave it to me on
  forget–me–not–square
For tunes never come my way
Cos they stopped all my pay,
And they took it away, on
  forget–me–not–square.

Their own version of another popular song went:

When they sound the last all-clear,
How happy I'm going to be,
No more 10A can stop my pay,
No sundeck party or clean ship that day.
From this ship I will depart,
And I won't be needing as start,
So, until that day,
They can keep all my pay
When they sound the last all-clear

Servicewomen, who used to march along the roads singing 'She'll be wearing khaki knickers when she comes', and members of the Women's Land Army, were just as keen as the men on singing parodies and popular and traditional songs at concerts and impromptu sing-songs in their Nissen huts with their neatly-folded sheets and blankets and their stacked 'biscuits'. Mrs Bett Spridgeon, of Whittlesey, Peterborough, earned twenty-two shillings for a forty-four hour week when she worked as a Land Girl from 1944 to 1950. She lived at one time in a hostel hutment for forty girls which had only one radio; the buses to the nearest town ran only every four hours. 'After a hard day's work', she writes, 'we often used to make our own entertainment by having a sing-song

An impromptu sing-song on
a minesweeper, 1942.

WAAFs practise tap dancing
in London, 1942.

round the old coke stove, while we were sitting up on our bunk beds. I got my mouth organ and the others had combs and paper or anything suitable and then we would start. Songs that we could harmonise to were our favourites; not that we were much good, but to our ears it sounded wonderful. We used to sing *Smile awhile, You are my Sunshine, Don't Fence me in, My baby has gone down the plughole, She's a Lassie from Lancashire,* etc.'

Mrs Withenshaw, who was stationed at Blacon Camp near Chester with the ATS, can still picture one girl who used to give a solo performance in their hut every night just before lights out. She would carry something over her shoulder in imitation of a gun and march up and down the hut in her pyjamas singing *There's something about a soldier.* Mrs Joan Kelly, of Fallowfield, Manchester, also remembers 'those happy years in the WAAF' and the songs they used to make up about themselves and their RAF colleagues:

I'll never forget the day, I enlisted on the spree,
To be a little WAAFy in the Royal WAAFery,
Now my heart is aching and is breaking
To see civilian life once more.
You should see the WAAFs on a Saturday night,
Polishing up their buttons in the pale moonlight,
For there's going to be inspection in the morning.
And the station warrant officer will be there,
He'll be there, he'll be there,
In his little wooden hut across the square,
While the WAAFs are all in order
He'll be kissing the CO's daughter
In his little wooden hut across the square.

Entertainers in grass skirts
get their cue.

CHAPTER 8

I WISH THAT I COULD HIDE INSIDE THIS LETTER

MANY of the songs of 1943, such as *Constantly, You'll never Know* and *Dearly Beloved*, were extremely romantic; but with hopes of ultimate victory in sight though still far distant there were some more optimistic songs such as *You'd be so nice to come home to* and *I'm going to get lit up (when the lights go up in London)*, which had been introduced by the vivacious Zoë Gail in *Strike a New Note* at the Prince of Wales Theatre in London. With these hints of final victory in the air, some of the top brass in the BBC had renewed doubts about its policy towards popular music, fearing, perhaps, that the wartime necessity of giving people what they wanted might set a precedent for peacetime, so that they tried to impose their own will once again.

Ever since the middle of the Twenties when Rudy Vallee had introduced crooning by singing through a megaphone, some people had always considered crooning to be morally reprehensible and effeminate. The BBC had made several attacks on it in pre-war days and in April, 1943, it decreed that one in three numbers in all broadcasts by dance bands should be non-vocal to prevent too much 'slush' and sentiment going out over the air. At the same time a number of vocalists were reported to have been banned from broadcasting altogether on the ground of their alleged incompetence.

In the previous year the BBC had set up an 'anti-slush' committee which wanted to stop all 'anaemic' performances by male vocalists and insincere or over-sentimental performances by women; and to ban any songs which were 'slushy' in sentiment, which contained innuendo, or which might offend against good taste, religion, or Allied susceptibilities. *Melody Maker* reported that sixteen numbers had been banned, including *I Try to say I love you, I'll just close my Eyes, So Deep is the Night, Miss You* and *Concerto for Two*! There were a number of other songs which upset the BBC during the war, including, for fairly obvious reasons, *Why don't we do this more often?* and *That Lovely Weekend*, which had been banned by some American radio stations because it did not state categorically that the couple involved were married! In December, 1943, the BBC imposed one of its silliest bans on the song *Paper Doll* because it thought that the emphasis on the fickleness of women might upset troops who were away from home; but the song was scarcely a novelty, having been published first during the First World War, without breaking too many hearts in the succeeding decades. Noël Coward's *Don't Let's Be Beastly to the Germans* was also banned for a time, apparently because some BBC officials did not understand that it was meant to be ironic. In 1944, *I Heard you Cried last night* was also prohibited for a time because it could imply that a man was crying.

The troops were neither so immature nor so vulnerable as some BBC officials thought. Knowing that their feelings required many different forms of release, they were not ashamed to indulge in sentiment or afraid to cry occasionally, in private at least. Mr Dennis Murray, of Littlemore, Oxford, remembers a concert party, led by Ralph Reader of *Gang Show* fame which he attended in a forward jungle position in Burma. 'He asked us to put our arms round the shoulders of the blokes on either side and to hum the tune *We'll Meet Again* whilst the first row swayed to the right, and the second row to the left and so on. The bamboo "basha" was full of brown, sweat-caked bodies swaying, and young faces smiling until Ralph started to tell us that one day we *would* again meet those we loved and had left behind so long ago. Everything went on just the same, except for the expression on the faces. There were so

many artificial smiles hiding, not very successfully, the fact that they were crying and trying not to in front of the boys.'

The powerlessness of the individual and the long years of enforced separation gave many men something to cry about at times. Mr J. Cocksey, of Wyth, Manchester, writes: 'Pining for a home-drafting to see my wife and kiddies again, I thought at long last that it had come when I was posted back to Malta from Augusta, Sicily, where I had spent the previous twelve months after the invasion of the island in 1943.

'My disappointment was profound when I found myself redrafted back to Taranto, Italy, attached to another naval party. I was billeted in the *Scuola Nuova*, a Taranto educational establishment. I shall never forget one evening. A little more "choka" [fed up] than usual, I was slouching up to our mess, a classroom. I was just about to enter, when from a wireless relay speaker came the sweetest (at that moment, particularly) voice in the world, the Forces Sweetheart, Our Vera, singing "There'll be bluebirds over . . ." and "Jimmy will go to sleep. . . ." (My eldest child was Jimmy!)

'I wiped away the tears before joining the mess. It wouldn't have done for a "killick" [petty officer] to have been seen crying.'

Songs from home, sentimental as they may now seem, and request programmes, whose participants often seemed inarticulate then were one of the most important factors in sustaining the morale of the fighting forces. Apart from its occasional silly bans of individual songs, the BBC did a magnificent job in providing these essential links between servicemen and women in all parts of the world and their relatives back home. In spite of staff shortages and limited resources, the BBC gradually developed the most comprehensive and longest daily short-wave service in the world with programmes being transmitted for twenty-two hours out of every twenty-four to all parts of the globe, from the south-west Pacific to North America and from India to the Continent of Europe. These programmes were different from the normal short-wave broadcasts which consisted mainly of news bulletins and of talks about Britain at war. They were specially designed for Forces overseas and provided much the same kind of entertainment as had originally been broadcast to the BEF in France.

The four stages in the build-up of the General Overseas Service were chronicled in the *BBC Year Book* for 1943. By Christmas, 1940, a special weekly programme was being broadcast to troops in India and others soon followed: to the RAF out East, to the Mediterranean Fleet, to Iceland, to the Tobruk garrison, to RAF aircrew being trained in Canada, to Malta, Gibraltar and Palestine. The second stage began as the armies started to pile up in the Middle East and in India with programmes being transmitted daily on the African and the Eastern services respectively. The next big step forward came in June, 1942, with the start of the General Overseas Service, which was beamed out to Forces in the Middle East for four hours each evening, though programmes were at first

Open air concerts for the troops
always drew a full house.

restricted to those being broadcast at the same time on other wavelengths. One of the first new series of simultaneous transmissions heard by men in the Middle East and their folks back home was *Introducing Anne*, featuring Anne Shelton and the Ambrose Players, which started on Sunday, 4 October 1942. The fourth stage came in November, 1942, when special Forces programmes consisting of music, light entertainment, news bulletins and occasional three-minute talks, were transmitted for seven hours a day. Finally, on 27 February 1944, the domestic Forces Programme was abolished and replaced by a General Forces Programme which could be heard by listeners overseas and at home.

One of the most important ingredients in these services were the message and request programmes. By 1942, there were fifty or sixty a week. Sandy Macpherson, the cinema organist, had been first off the mark with *Sandy Calling* and his was followed by many more. *Your Cup of Tea*, run by Freddie Grisewood, is still remembered by Eighth Army veterans to whom it was beamed: *Over to You* brings back memories of training in Canada for RAF aircrew; *Home Town*, introduced by the cheery voice of Ronnie Shiner, is still recollected by those who served on the George Cross island of Malta; and men who served at sea still remember their own programme, *Blue Peter*. The most popular programme of this kind was Vera Lynn's programme, *Sincerely Yours*, which started in November, 1941, and was produced, as was *The Brains Trust*, by Howard Thomas.

Although the chance of your number coming up on a request programme was almost as remote as winning the pools—which had become the Unity Pools for the duration—these programmes were listened to avidly by millions of people all over the world for the chance of hearing a message or a song from someone they loved. Mr S. Rigney, of Hyde, Cheshire, will never forget his happiness when he heard a request for him in the Cotton Tree Club, Ismailia. 'Just as I had got my sausage and chips, it came over the speakers, a request on my behalf from Vera Lynn—*Memories live Longer than Dreams*. As I had not seen my eldest daughter at all, and my wife for two years, it was appropriate.'

For millions of listeners, Vera Lynn's programme was one of the high spots of the week. Mr Norman Gardiner, of Southampton, who was stationed at RAF Cardington, writes: 'Every time now when I hear the voice of Vera Lynn, either on radio, television or records, singing *Yours, We'll Meet Again* and especially *The White Cliffs of Dover*, I am immediately transported back in time to a hut on that station with all my old mates of those days, listening with rapt attention and in absolute silence (a rare happening in a billet full of airmen), to Vera singing those songs over the wireless.

'Most evenings nearly all the occupants, save for a few who would be writing letters home, were away down to Bedford, over at the Naafi, or at the station cinema; but if someone was heard to say, "Vera's on tonight", then every occupant of the hut would remain in, all lying on their beds listening to her. It is a memory of those days, and of those songs, that I shall never forget.'

Writing the first Christmas card
home.

Visits by ENSA artists did even more to boost the troops' morale: the lonely figure of a girl vocalist in evening dress, shaded by a hastily erected awning from the desert sun and protected from enemy aircraft by gunners, reassured the sunburnt, weary, lonely men, sitting on their upturned petrol cans, that there was still an England and that someone back there still cared. During the war ENSA gave over two and a half million entertainments of all kinds, from film shows to concerts by top artists, from elaborate gala performances to solo performances by unknowns in the open air. 'The ENSA badge was everywhere', wrote Basil Dean in *The Theatre at War*. 'Beginning as a side decoration on hundreds of stages and platforms in camp and factory and over the doorways of requisitioned houses and offices, it had quickly spread to foreign lands. Affixed to the façades of theatres and cinemas, adorning the sides of lorries, coaches and trucks as they bumped and hurtled themselves over the desert roads of Libya or the *corniches* of Italy, or the jungle tracks of Burma, or proceeding more sedately along the boulevards of capital cities—everywhere the red, white and blue badge of ENSA entertainment was to be seen.'

Dance bands, vocalists, actors, actresses, entertainers shared all the discomforts and dangers of desert and jungle, often giving impromptu, additional shows at forward air strips in breaks on their long and arduous journeys. Many of them had narrow escapes. Geraldo and some members of his orchestra were involved in a serious air crash when they were flying over Italy in 1943 on their way to a lengthy tour of the Middle East, which would include North Africa, Syria and Palestine. They were only saved by the skill of the American pilot who made a successful crash landing in a muddy field in the mountains. Joe Loss, who had been one of the first band leaders to visit the BEF in France during the phoney war was one of the first to go back again with a sixteen-piece band to entertain the BLA after the Normandy invasion.

Even in peacetime the commercial face of show business always wears a charitable grin which expanded into a benevolent smile during the war when there was a much more general sense of service and of duty among all kinds and classes of people. In March, 1940, for example, the Dutch who were still merrily booking British dance bands as if the phoney war would never cease, invited Harry Roy to make a short tour of their country; but he turned the offer down in the belief that it was his duty to play only to British audiences in wartime and not to neutrals as the Dutch still were until the Germans invaded their country two months later.

Apart from these rare visitations by ENSA artists and the BBC's request programmes, men serving overseas had no other links with home but for letters. From the very beginning of the war, the

Letters to folks back home often demanded much thought.

A message from Normandy, 1944.

Service women stationed overseas get
their mail from home.

art of letter-writing, which was already disappearing, was temporarily revived not as a literary form but as an essential means of communication for millions of ordinary men and women who laboured at their daily compositions more diligently than they had ever done at school. Many people wrote at least one letter every day for many years: they were not brief postcard scrawls but often long epistles. In a book of tributes, *Sweethearts All*, compiled by the *Sunday Pictorial* at the end of the war, one airman said that his girl-friend had written to him every day since he had joined up. On average, she wrote six or seven pages, but occasionally as many as seventeen. A corporal, whose wife was serving on an ack-ack site somewhere in England while he was otherwise engaged in Europe, said that his wife still found time, in spite of her duties, to write to him nearly every day and she often sent him 'words of songs or poems that express the way she feels for me'. Many servicemen carried verses in their jacket pocket or their writing case as a talisman. Mrs M. Whyatt, of Reddish, Stockport, Cheshire, was a nineteen-year-old war-bride in 1940. On her husband's embarkation leave they saw their last film together, which was called *Seventh Heaven* and featured the song *My Diane*. Her husband said that if they ever had children, the first girl would be called Diane. Some time later, Mrs Whyatt found the words of the song, and sent them to him. Four-and-a-half years later, when they met again, she found the words of the song in the cover of his writing case, which he had carried everywhere with him through the battle of El Alamein and all the subsequent campaigns. (Their first child was born in

1946, a girl, called Diane.)

For many men and women the daily writing of those letters became a self-educative process which allowed them to explore previously concealed realms of thought and feeling in themselves and in others. 'I found out more about myself and my real feelings by writing all those letters', one former Army sergeant writes, 'than I had ever done in ten years of work and marriage before the war.' The wide range of occupations and educational achievement in most Nissen huts and mess decks meant that no one was ever at a loss for words. There was usually one man, better educated than the rest, who performed a similar function to a medieval scribe, reading letters to illiterates and writing their replies. 'I remember one bloke', a sailor writes, 'who was a walking dictionary. He could write such hot love letters that he was always in demand, especially if one of his mates had had a tiff with his wife or sweetheart.' For those who had no girl-friend, there were many organisations which could supply the name of a pen-pal. In October, 1940, the British Legion (as it then was) had set up a special section to check on the credentials of female pen-friends to guard against spies, 'undesirable women' and 'hero-worshipping girls', while the commanding officers vouched for the honour of their troops.

The arrival of a letter whose envelope had been inscribed with SWALK (Sealed with a Loving Kiss) or of an airgraph—a miniature photographic reproduction of a one-page letter—were one of the most eagerly awaited occasions in the war, just as the delivery of an official telegram was one of the most dreaded. There was quite a scandal in 1944 when it was revealed that airmail letters to Ceylon, which cost one shilling and sixpence, a lot of money for a soldier's wife, travelled most of the way by sea, being flown on only when they had reached Egypt. As a result, air letters took fourteen days to reach Colombo, while a surface letter took two months and a parcel up to six. As postal services had such a low priority, letters often arrived in batches, weeks late or out of sequence, so that order had to be restored by a re-reading. These little censored scraps of paper were read and read again in an imaginative attempt to recreate the described experience that the distant partner could not share. Jealous men suffered agonies of apprehension as their passion fed on some apparently suspicious name or phrase, until a subsequent letter reassured them temporarily or, sometimes, confirmed all their worst fears. The importance of letters from home was officially recognised by the Morale (Far Eastern) Inter-Services Committee, which had asked the Ministry of Information to see if women's magazines could persuade their readers to write more frequently to men in the 'Forgotten Army' in the Far East. On 27 July 1945, it was reported to the committee that the MOI had been successful in its task: 'Stress had been laid on the desirability not only of frequent letters, but also cheerful ones.' For years millions of men and women had had to live with written images and abstractions: the general yearning for something more tangible was summed up in one song title of 1944, *I wish that I could Hide inside this Letter*, which expressed a universal wish.

'It's a boy!' Good news from home.

CHAPTER 9

THIS IS THE ARMY, MR. JONES

FOR many fighting men forbidden to keep diaries, which might have been of use to the enemy if they were captured, songs and visits by ENSA artists chronicled the course of their individual wartime odyssey, rising up as rare peaks of delight above the blurred confusion of battle. Mr Self, of Alton, who remembered hearing *A Nightingale Sang in Berkeley Square* in the blitzed city of Portsmouth, has some particularly precise memories of this kind:

Yours and *We'll Meet Again*
A Toc H concert on the beaches of the Arakan coast, 28 April 1944. A concert by Vera Lynn. I could not get inside the hall, so I stood by the window—a cooler spot than inside. I still have the souvenir of a rupee note signed by Vera herself, the night she was adopted as 'The Sweetheart of the Fighting Fourteenth Army'.

All Hail the Power of Jesu's Name
Community singing at the Presbyterian Church Rest Room, Calcutta, December, 1944.

A Journey to a Star
Sung by Alice Faye in a film show near Kohima, December 1944, with the hills and the jungle all around and the stars bright overhead.

When Day is Done
As sung by Valerie, an ENSA artist, in the ruins of Nyaungu, Burma, 1945.

Particular songs can still recall for individuals similar experiences which were shared by many thousands or millions of fighting men during the war. No one who ever docked at Durban in a troopship will ever forget their first relieved sight of the coastline after what had often been a hazardous journey or some of the first sounds of South Africa, blown hither and thither by the winds, which were eventually seen to emanate from a large woman dressed in white whose words gradually became more distinguishable as the ship approached the port. Perla Siedle, a retired Wagnerian soprano, welcomed 5,000 Allied ships during the war, singing *Land of Hope and Glory* for the British and *God Bless America* for the Americans. For most servicemen and women she was anonymous then and has remained so ever since; but her singing still brings back memories of one of the great folk experiences of the war. Reactions to the event varied. Alan Jenkins writes in *The Forties*: 'We wept, because she was Mother, because we had been so lonely.' But the present writer's experience was different. On my troopship, most of the men, a sterner crowd perhaps, were initially bewildered and then embarrassed and finally amused or overcome with

Vera Lynn on her triumphal
tour of the Far East.

laughter. The subsequent reaction to Durban itself was more uniform: the frantic dash towards early-closing bars after weeks of abstinence in a troopship; the feasting upon huge piles of unrationed fruit at unbelievably low prices; the wondrous excitement at huge cars running freely again. The whole event became encapsulated in the minds of many hundreds of thousands of people as one of the unforgettable wartime experiences.

There were many other shared, song-centred memories of a similar kind which in aggregate compose the collective consciousness which makes one history of the war. Troopships with their bawdy sing-songs and their endless games of cards or housey-housey ('Seven and six—was she worth it?') aroused much emotion as the long hours of enforced inactivity on the voyage into the unknown or on the journey back to more familiar places, allowed feelings of anticipation to well up from the unconscious. Mr Norman Howes to Totton, Southampton, writes:

I was a sergeant in the 2nd BN South Staffordshire Regiment, a glider-borne battalion of the 1st Airborne Division, and early in 1944 we were on a troopship, the *Duchess of Bedford*, en route from North Africa back to Blighty.

We had taken part in the airborne invasion of Sicily and later the seaborne invasion of Italy and were on our way back to re-form, and to re-train reinforcements, ready, as we now know, to be nearly annihilated in the battle of Arnhem. One day out of Gibraltar our ship was in severe collision with another troopship, the *Monarch of Bermuda*, which was last seen listing heavily and being escorted back to Gibraltar; but strangely this is my secondary memory of the journey.

Soon after we left North Africa, they started a record request programme over the ship's intercom and one of the first records played was Mary Martin singing *Do it Again* with the refrain 'DO DO DO DO IT AGAIN.'

I can still remember the shipful of ardent heterosexuals, on their way back to wives and sweethearts, drooling over these words and the anguished, frustrated groans that greeted the record as it was requested all day and every day of the journey home.

The Maori farewell song, *Now is the Hour*, brings back an 'unforgettable memory' for Captain H. R. Gibbs of Brentwood, Essex:
We were aboard the P. & O. ship, the *Strathaird*, pressed into service as a trooper, bound for India. The ship berthed at Aden to take on a New Zealand Maori battalion, who were heading for home, having completed their 'stint' in the Middle East.

A night or two after we left Aden, these lads treated us to an impromptu concert under the stars. As their voices rang out across the water, the feeling of nostalgia was all-embracing, and it culminated in their singing their own farewell song. It brought a lump to many a throat. For a brief hour or so, these lads, by their own brand of magic, had taken us all away from the thoughts of the unknown which lay ahead of us, whilst they themselves were heading for home.

Ports and harbours, those great repositories of collective emotions of joy and sadness since the beginning of human history, captured the imagination of many thousands of civilians turned sailors for the duration. Mr J. German, of Romiley, Stockport, served at one time with a flotilla of Lease-Lend American destroyers based at Londonderry. 'The song that brings back wartime memories', he writes, 'is the picture in my mind of a barefooted Irish boy on the quayside of Londonderry harbour, singing the song called, I believe, *A Mother's Love's a Blessing* which finishes with the words "you'll never miss your mother till she's buried beneath the clay". His song would bring a throwing

down of pennies as a collection for the boy.' The memory of similar barefooted beggars, Irish, Egyptian, Indian, Arab, became part of the collective experience of thousands of men and women serving overseas.

A very different kind of song recalls the atmosphere of an Eastern port one night for Mr F. G. Allen of Norwich. 'I suppose it must have been in '45 that we had anchored in Hollandia, on the northern coast of New Guinea', he writes. 'It was hot and still. There were some twenty American boats scattered around, all flashing Morse; there were fireflies flittering around. Then one of the Yanks put on *Hawaiian War Chant*, very loud, and it was just right. I was on *HMS Lothian*, a converted banana boat, the HQ ship of Force X sent out to help in the war against Japan; but, in fact, we never did more than cruise round the islands.'

Songs help to recall the boredom of war for many men. Mr Les Porteous, of Manchester, remembers how 'half-a-dozen of us lads on a day's leave in Cairo from our unit in the desert, entered the Diana cinema to find a full house. However, the manager fixed us up with a box; but the picture being shown was very boring and I was becoming restless when, through the open sides of the cinema, came the strains of *Deep in the Heart of Texas*. I joined in with gusto, clapping my hands at the appropriate time. How I enjoyed that barrel organ; but not the bashing I got from my mates!'

Mr Clifford Walker of Kidderminster, went into the RAF in May, 1941, when he was nineteen and was posted to Padgate where he spent ten boring days, confined with other recruits

Sailors waiting at Algiers, 1943.

to camp. He was pleased to be posted with two hundred other 'erks' to Bridlington. As they were passing the Humber, he was standing in the corridor watching the current agitating the weeds near the bank. At that moment a group of 'erks' in a nearby compartment started to sing *Tumbling Tumbleweeds*. 'I occasionally play the record nowadays', he writes, 'and it never fails to evoke memories of those far-off mid-war years.'

Other tunes symbolised whole campaigns for thousands of men then as they still do for many men and women in Britain and allied countries to this day. *J'Attendrai* brings back vivid memories of the invasion of Europe for Mr T. Coyne, of Shaw, Lancashire, who served with the 33rd Field Regiment, 3rd British Infantry Division. 'On 6 June 1978,' he writes, 'I was singing it again with five Frenchmen, one Dutchman, two Dutch ladies, five Englishmen and two Englishwomen in a French hotel ten yards from the landing memorial at Le Breche in Normandy,' and wishing that he had a tape recorder as he still does not have a record.

Another tune brings back similar memories of those same 'days of uncertainty' for Mr F. C. Wadsworth of Swindon, who served as a sapper with HQ, No. 2 Railway Construction and Maintenance Group, RE. 'Whilst stationed in Bayeux in August, 1944, soon after the establishment of the Second Front, I was allocated a seat in the gallery of the local theatre with others of my unit to see a play (the name of which I cannot now remember) starring Diana Wynyard and Ivor Novello.* During the interval, Mr Novello went down to the orchestra pit, sat down at the grand piano, and played and sang a song which he had just written, but which he had not then given a title. The eventual name of that song? *We'll Gather Lilacs*, of course! As this song attained its world-wide popularity, I have thought of this many

* It was *Love from a Stranger*.

163

times and its association with those days of uncertainty.'

The grim ironies of war, fortuitous or created, never failed to impress events on the memory. Mr J. L. Cull, of Oldham, was a radio operator in the 'few square yards of hell' at Arnhem. 'After a particularly bad night of heavy shelling and mortar fire, I was asked by lads in the immediate vicinity to try to get the news on my radio set. I tuned in to the BBC and the announcer said: "You have been listening to Frank Sinatra's latest record, *I couldn't sleep a wink last Night*".'

But the song above all others that evokes the most emotive memories of the war is *We'll Meet Again* with its striking contrast between sentiment and reality. For Mr Ernest H. Green, of Chislehurst, Kent, it recalls being stationed in the Orkneys and not knowing if his family who had just been bombed in Balham, London, were still safe.

For Mr G. Edwardson, of Altrincham, Cheshire, it brings back memories of RAF low-level bombers heading into the flak which came up 'like a steel curtain' around Caen in 1945 while he wondered how many of them would ever meet again.

Mr John Harris, of Northendon, near Manchester, will always remember the time when his ship, the *Barham*, was torpedoed on 15 November 1941, at 4.15 a.m. As it went down with 'a few hundred men', the survivors could hear *We'll Meet Again* coming over the internal loudspeakers.

Mr E. Lunt, MM, secretary of the Bolton and District Far Eastern Prisoner of War Association, recollects it being sung at the departmental mess in Singapore 'at the very last social evening before the Nips closed in on us'. It continued to be sung at impromptu concerts during his years of captivity as a prisoner of war and helped to keep up the spirits of the 'lucky people who came back from hell after four years with the Nips'.

Songs did a great deal to sustain morale among prisoners of war in the Far East, and in Germany where there were much greater chances of organising regular entertainment. By 1 January 1944, *Melody Maker* reported, virtually every POW camp in Germany had its own band or orchestra. One large camp had such a highly organised entertainments section that it even sent out dance bands and concert parties to tour satellite working-party sites in transport provided by the Germans. Most of the instruments and the sheet music were provided through the Red Cross. Mr Bruce, of Moss Side, Manchester, who was captured in France in 1940, was held in Stalag XXA and Stalag XXB, before he was repatriated with other wounded and chronic sick in 1943. He still remembers the 'great shows' that were put on at Marienburg (XXB), but one incident at the beginning of his captivity in Stalag XXA remains even more vivid in his memory. 'A big Cockney soldier got as many men together as possible, and in open defiance of our captors, sang with great gusto *There'll always be an England, Roll out the Barrel, Tipperary* and *Pack up Your Troubles*.' These same songs of defiance echoed loudly in many other prisoner of war compounds in times of trouble or unbearable exasperation, bringing hope and joy to those who were fortunate enough to survive the rigours of captivity.

164

CHAPTER 10

SHINE ON VICTORY MOON

BY 1944, although heavy fighting continued on all fronts and London had been subjected to renewed aerial attacks by Hitler's secret weapons—V1 flying bombs and V2 rockets—victory felt much closer and the songs of the year reflected this new promise. Songwriters produced some predictable numbers, which always mark the approaching end of any war, such as *Shine on Victory Moon, Victory Polka* and *When we Dance at the Victory Ball*; and others of a more personal, but still optimistic note, like *I'm going to build a Future World (Around You)* and *When the Great New World is Dawning*. But none of these was nearly as popular as one avowedly silly song with a refrain as 'nutty as a fruit cake'—*Mairzy Doats and Dozy Doats (Mares Eat Oats and Does Eat Oats)*.

Mairzy doats and dozy doats and liddle lamzy divey
A kiddley divey, too, wouldn't you?

People listened, intent and breathless, with their ear right up against the fretted aperture of the loudspeaker to catch the few silly words of which the refrain was composed, while the publishers rubbed their hands with glee as the sales of sheet music soared into six figures. The song reintroduced into the grim and purposeful wartime scene something of the pre-war frivolity and insouciance for which people increasingly yearned, just as Cole Porter's *Don't Fence Me In* expressed their desire for an end to wartime restrictions and discipline.

There had as yet been little real relief for either fighting men or civilians; but on 17 September 1944, there came a welcome change when the universally detested black-out was replaced by a dim-out, which allowed people, except for those living on the coast, to use normal curtains again. By the end of the year, ARP masks on car headlights had been abolished and lighting in trains, trams and buses was back to its pre-war intensity again, though it was not until 24 April 1945, that all lighting restrictions were totally abolished but for a narrow coastal strip. Neon signs, unused since

Allied troops celebrate the
liberation of Belgium.

the beginning of the war, flashed again in city streets and shop windows blazed with light fulfilling all the hopes that had been repeatedly expressed in song from *Till the Lights of London Shine Again* in 1940 to *I'm going to get lit up (When the Lights go Up in London)* of 1943.

The songs of 1945 were somewhat undistinguished apart from Ivor Novello's *We'll Gather Lilacs*, which repeated for him the great success he had with *Keep the Home Fires Burning* during the First World War. The song-writers were exhausted, having said it all; but that didn't matter as they had already written many numbers which were still popular and people would create their own celebrations when victory came. During the last great battles in western Europe, soldiers of the BLA had shared in all the excitement and relief of their continental allies who had been freed

from years of Nazi occupation and oppression. Paris was liberated on 25 August 1944, among scenes of heartfelt joy and celebration, with Parisians singing the *Marseillaise*, shouting 'Vive la France' and dancing with happiness in the flag-bedecked streets. Brussels was freed shortly afterwards on 3 September and Amsterdam was liberated on 5 May 1945. In every liberated city and town British soldiers were kissed and hugged and their victorious tanks were covered with flowers—and with girls.

But even these great celebrations of joy were surpassed in London when the war in Europe finally ended after 2,094 days—526 days longer than the First World War. VE day was officially celebrated on Tuesday, 8 May 1945; but Londoners who had been waiting the whole of the previous day for it to be announced, went wild with joy when it

166

VE celebrations in
Leicester Square.

was stated officially at 7.30 on Monday evening that VE day would be celebrated the following day. By 9 p.m. the streets of the West End were impenetrably crowded with hundreds of thousands of civilians and servicemen of many nationalities, Australians in their slouch hats, French sailors in their black berets and red pom poms and the ever-present GIs. Flags waved; rockets exploded in the skies; bonfires blazed on blitz sites and in the streets. Huge crowds with linked arms marched and counter-marched up and down the wide streets leading towards Buckingham Palace singing *Bless 'Em All, Roll out the Barrel* and *Tipperary*. In Leicester Square, hundreds of servicemen and civilians joined in *Knees Up Mother Brown* to the sounds of a barrel organ; and later a Guards officer and an American girl led a twisting, shouting, singing line of thousands in a massive conga which snaked its way across the whole square. In the Haymarket, a huge bonfire was lit after midnight, while thousands stood around it singing *There'll always be an England*. Cars were swallowed up by the immense crowds so that their drivers were forced to abandon their vehicles and to join in the celebrations: a bus which was trying to edge its way through the crowds of people, had two sailors, three soldiers and four airmen dancing on its roof.

There was scarcely any respite in this spontaneous outbreak of happiness and joy before the official celebrations started the next day. Winston Churchill made the official announcement on the radio at 3 p.m.; but he also appeared on the balcony of the Ministry of Health in Whitehall to speak to the vast crowds below. 'This is your victory', he told them. 'It is not the victory of a party, or of any class or section of the community. It is the victory of the great British nation as a whole.' The cinemas in the West End were closed, though the theatres stayed open. Restaurants were packed and so were the dance halls. At the Hammersmith Palais the doors were shut again almost as soon as they were opened: the music of Lou Praeger and Jack Amlott was relayed to the people on the pavements outside. At the YMCA centre in central London, there was a special Victory dance for servicemen and women where discipline still prevailed with all of the men wearing full uniform and only some of the Service women dancing jacketless in rolled-up shirt sleeves. Public houses were allowed to stay open to midnight. Although they were packed, no one really needed any artificial stimulus to celebrate and to dance and sing and laugh with total abandon in the streets.

Crowds of men and women marched and counter-marched again through the wide streets where they were not too densely packed with people. The London correspondent of the *Manchester Guardian* (as it then was) made one interesting point. He noted that there were many groups of ATS and WAAF, Land Army girls in shirts and breeches and typists and office girls in civilian clothes marching along and singing 'without a man among them', and commented perceptively: 'No doubt uniformed service has produced in many girls a group spirit and a new feeling of their value and independence as women—and, incidentally, a habit of community singing. As for the non-uniformed girls, one contributory cause may be that so many more of them

are now economically independent and have got into the habit of looking after themselves.'

Hundreds of thousands of people converged on Buckingham Palace shouting 'We want the king', who had been transformed by war from a shy, stammering man who did not really want to be king into the democratic leader of a nation which he had helped to unite by his example of sacrifice, hard work and resolution. For two hours every night he put on overalls to work at a bench making

The Fleet's lit up.

munitions and, although it was not generally known to his people then, he always carried with him, wherever he went, a plain wooden case, containing his own personal Sten gun to use against any invader.

Outside the palace that night, there was a spontaneous display of loyalty and affection which has been repeated in the post-war years only during the celebrations of the present Queen's jubilee, recalling for those who can remember the Victory days something of the old wartime spirit. Half-an-hour after midnight, King George VI and Queen Elizabeth (the Queen Mother), joined by Churchill and other members of the royal family including the present Queen in her ATS uniform, had appeared on the floodlit balcony of Buckingham Palace for the eighth time. The crowds would have let them go on appearing all night.

There were also wild rejoicings in other cities. Glasgow, like London, could not wait for the official celebrations and on Monday night, George Square was packed tight with a huge crowd of

whole, celebrations in most provincial cities were far less riotous and wild than they were in London, though there was singing, dancing, cheering—and street parties for children—everywhere. At Worthing, Sussex, there was a VE tea-dance in the Assembly Hall, followed by another victory dance in the evening; people danced in Bank Park, Warrington, which had been decorated with fairy lights for the occasion; and in Plymouth 1,000 couples danced again on the Hoe, as others had done during the

Flags and rosettes welcomed victory.

civilians and servicemen estimated to total a hundred thousand. Pipers were out in the city streets which had already been decorated with flags, bunting and streamers. In Liverpool, on the following day, there was organised street dancing in Hamilton Square; many streets had bonfire parties and most of them burnt effigies of Hitler. In Manchester, the 150-foot-long entrance to Belle Vue was decorated with Allied flags and surmounted by an illuminated V-sign composed of red, white and blue lamps. Dancing went on till 2 a.m. But, on the

blitz, watched by a crowd of about 20,000 spectators.

Although the war was over in Europe, it still continued in the East. The myth of Japanese invincibility had at last been destroyed. Rangoon, the capital of Burma, had been re-taken on 2 May 1945, but there was still a vast mopping-up operation to be done, which was made doubly difficult by the nature of the terrain and by the monsoon.

Now that the war had ended in Europe, more attention could be paid to the needs of the Fourteenth, or Forgotten

169

Army, the biggest single army of the Second World War which, with all its ancillary formations, totalled nearly a million men. Compared with troops in most other theatres of war, these men had long lacked even the most elementary comforts. These deficiencies were recognised in an interim report of 20 June 1944, of the Morale (Far Eastern) Inter-Services Committee, which had been set up earlier in the year under the chairmanship of Brigadier E. H. A. J. O'Donnell.

India has certain disadvantages as a base from the morale and welfare points of view. . . . The cities provide indifferent, expensive and often demoralising forms of recreation, and the leave camps leave much to be desired. There is very little white female population. . . . The attitude of the white population of India to the Services, so we are told, leaves much to be desired. . . . Troops in South-East Asia (other than naval personnel in ships) are badly provisioned with wireless sets, and with suitable programmes to which to listen. Because of the fading which is inherent in short-wave transmission, the General Forces Programme can only be satisfactorily received on good sets. All-India Radio devotes all but a small portion of the day to broadcasts in the vernacular or of matters of no interest to the troops.

The committee recommended that improvements should be made in both the quality and the quantity of concert parties sent out to the area, and that more radios and gramophones should be provided.

By 10 June 1945, there were 259 ENSA artistes and 172 local artistes at work in India and South-east Asia Command; an RAF band of twenty-four players was on its way to India; and a Royal Marines orchestra was due to leave shortly for a six-month tour. By August, the first of the promised 15,000 gramophones had been delivered, but the rest arrived too late for use during the war.

On 6 August 1945, the first atomic bomb was exploded over Hiroshima and the second over Nagasaki three days later. The Japanese surrendered on Tuesday, 14 August but owing to the need to synchronise the announcements from London, Washington, Moscow and Chungking, it was midnight before the new British Prime Minister, Mr Attlee, announced that the victory over Japan and the end of the Second World War would be celebrated by public holidays on 15 and 16 August.

Because of the lateness of the hour, there were far fewer unofficial celebrations than there had been on the night before VE day, though some people, particularly in Glasgow, did get up again to celebrate. Miss N. Coward, of Poole, Dorset, had no need to do so as she was working on the night shift in a munitions factory at the time. 'We went berserk', she writes. 'We all left our machines. There was a box of theatrical costumes at the back of the factory stage and I dressed up as a ballet dancer and did my best to do the dying-swan act. Several of us donned all sorts of costumes and, with complete abandon, cavorted about the stage. All our pent-up emotions were released. After a couple of hours the management ordered us back on the shop floor. Many people thought we must have had a couple of pints to drink, but it was

170

completely spontaneous.'

Throughout the country, but particularly in London, the next two days were given over to the wildest party that the country had ever seen since 18 and 19 May 1900, when Mafeking had been relieved during the Boer War. Most reports agree that the crowds were even bigger and more unruly than on VE night. Guardsmen hurtled down Whitehall Place on roller skates; girls were tossed up into the air by joyous crowds to land elsewhere, often injured; over 200 people were hurt by fireworks in London alone. Civilians and troops wearing paper hats sang all the wartime favourites and danced everything from the *Can Can* to *Knees up Mother Brown*. From the balcony of the American Red Cross, the Rainbow Club Orchestra gave a free concert for the huge crowd of many nationalities down below, while, inside, everything was on the house.

Mrs Alice Solomon, of Brandon, near Durham, was living at that time in Shepperton, Middlesex, where Alan Breeze, who had sung with Billy Cotton's band since 1932, also lived. She recalls that there were bonfires in the street and singing in the church hall, led by Alan Breeze who sang *Yours* and *The White Cliffs of Dover*. In all parts of the country, the pubs were packed. For Mrs M. Holmes, the song *Five Minutes More* always brings back memories of VJ night. 'We had a party at the Manor House. It was some party. Every time the landlord called time, we sang *Give us Five Minutes More*. In the end, the landlord and his wife went to bed at three o'clock in the morning and left us to it. But we all went down before opening time on the next morning (or the same morning) and cleaned up for them.'

Allied celebrations in London on VE day.

171

CHAPTER 11

I'M GONNA LOVE THAT GUY

WITH the euphoria of victory and all its joyous celebrations past, there began for most men the most frustrating period of their lives in the Services: the seemingly interminable wait in Britain for their discharge and the even longer delays overseas before a troopship or a plane took them back home again. Men who were already on embarkation leave on VJ day were given an extra two days' furlough before they were sent overseas. To avoid the flooding of the labour market by ex-servicemen which had occurred after the First World War, releases from the Forces were rigidly controlled. Most men were discharged on an age and service basis under Class A, while a smaller number were released earlier under Class B if they possessed skills essential for 'national reconstruction' or under Class C on extreme compassionate grounds. At the demobilisation centre, they were kitted out with a free set of civilian clothes, though they retained their uniform as they were officially liable to recall until the 'emergency' was ended by Order in Council. They were given part of the pay due to them for their final leave and credited with their gratuity and post-war credits which in the case of a private with five years' service amounted to the munificent sum of £61 18s. 6d. (Officers did little better: a major received a gratuity of £111.) Then they started on their journey home, travelling on a free railway warrant for the last time, to try to pick up the threads of their lives again, which had often been broken by five or six years of separation. For many men and women it was one of the most traumatic experiences of their lives.

Fighting men from overseas, still trying to live out the delayed shock of warfare through their endless reminiscences, returned to find an England which had altered immeasurably in many ways since they had been away. The photographs they had seen could give no full indication of the havoc that enemy bombs, pilotless planes and rockets had wreaked in the interval. Their eyes were long accustomed to destruction, but of other people's homes, not their own. In every city, many of the old familiar landmarks had gone or they survived as charred and blackened skeletons of cathedrals, churches, guildhalls, office blocks, department stores and town halls rising up above the piles of still uncleared debris. Scarcely any houses had been repaired; shop windows were shattered. The paint was peeling everywhere and most things wore a dingy air. Civilians, who had fought their own war, were accustomed to these sights and even proud of the scars which showed their suffering; but returning servicemen, without this experience and this conditioning, found England dingy, shabby, devastated.

There had been equivalent changes in society. The disruption of family life, the long years of separation, the forced gaiety of wartime had taken a heavy toll. Even by October, 1940, there had been increasing public concern about 'shelter girls' in Liverpool and some other big cities, who rarely slept at home, but spent the nights in street air-raid shelters, drinking, dancing, and going with men until the dawn. By 1941, there had been an increase in the number of cases of syphilis of at least 50 per cent. and of at least 70 per cent. if the Services were included, compared with pre-war. There were many lost legions of children, who had been abandoned by their mothers, and had returned to their cities from the reception areas to live in gangs in bombed houses. The number of spivs had multiplied; there were thousands of deserters on the run. The amount spent on drink and tobacco had increased enormously. Some wives had found other lovers during their husband's absence; others did not wish to resume their relationship. Many fighting men returned

An officer being measured for his new
suit at Olympia.

173

from overseas to find grown children whom they had never seen and, in some cases, had never even fathered. They also brought back their own secrets. Even servicemen who never left the shores of Britain had found it difficult to see much of their wives and families owing to the lack of free time and the partiality of posting officers for stationing servicemen miles away from home. One contributor

'WARE SHARKS
TAKE CARE OF YOUR GRATUITY

GET INDEPENDENT EXPERT ADVICE ON ANY SEEMINGLY ATTRACTIVE OFFERS OF
EMPLOYMENT WITH INVESTMENT, OR OF SMALL SHOPS AND BUSINESSES

An official warning to demobbed servicemen.

to the *Sunday Pictorial* anthology, Sgt L. K. N. Newling, kept a careful note of his wartime journeys and calculated that in his five years in the RAF he had to travel 'a distance of 18,084 miles by rail, 5,000 miles by cycle, 1,400 miles by car, 500 miles by bus, and 50 miles on foot, a grand total of 24,900 miles,' equivalent to a circumnavigation of the globe, just to spend a few brief hours with his wife on his weekly free days. Everyone was now a stranger.

For many people, however, all the promises of their shared songs and hopes were instantly fulfilled in the spontaneous joys of their reunion. For the first six years of her married life, Mrs May Insley of Salford, Lancs, had literally nothing but *That Lovely Weekend* to remember:

I haven't said thanks for that lovely
  weekend,
Those two days of heaven you helped me
  to spend,
The thrill of your kiss as you stepped off
  the train,
The smile in your eyes like the sun after
  rain.

She was married on 10 June 1939, after her husband, a reservist, had already received his call-up papers. 'We did have a nice weekend together and went to work on Monday, 12 June—Tuesday—Wednesday—then Thursday, 15 June he went into the Army. He was sent to Malta for four-and-a-half-years and spent the next one-and-a-half years in Italy and Africa, returning on 3 April 1945. I was too upset, both of us were, to part so soon, and every time I hear that song after thirty-nine years of married life, I still sing it with tears in my eyes.'

Mrs Nancy Mavis Senior, of Bristol, remembers *Amapola* most of all the wartime tunes 'because the last line was "I love you" and this was the only way I could tell my sweetheart how I did love him, as I was only fifteen. He went to France and I waited two years for him to come home, not a fit man. We wrote daily to each other and have just celebrated our thirty-second wedding anniversary.'

'Yes, I have memories, too', says Mrs I. Gibson, of Sunderland. 'Our only son was a prisoner-of-war of the Japanese and for over two years we did not know if he was alive as he was only posted missing. Finally we were told he had been captured at Singapore. The ship was bombed and they had to swim for their lives. He had sung in a choir since he was eight and even when he was on leave he would do so. The last solo he sang was *Hear My Prayer*. At nights I would stand in my backyard, pick out a star and say "Hear my Prayer". The Lord did hear my prayer and sent our son back to us.'

Other reunions did not last for many years. That song, *We'll Meet Again*, which had just as big an impact on civilians as on servicemen, still brings back memories of those bitterly deceptive years for Mrs Pat Gorner, of Southampton. 'My husband was overseas for six long years; our son was just a baby then. Vera Lynn's song *We'll Meet Again* made me cry. It still does, for Bill came home all right. Just two years later, I was told that he had three years to live, which he did. Once again, I was on my own with my thirteen-year-old son.' The same song evokes similar feelings for Mrs Dickens, of Corby, whose husband, Dix, had been posted back briefly from India before he was sent out to the Far East again, where he was transferred from the 17th–21st Lancers to the mechanised Royal Sussex Regiment. It was the last song he sang to her as they were walking back to their billets on the final night of his embarkation leave; and the first she heard him singing when he returned home again after more than five years. She got a message over the radio saying that he was coming home and went to meet his troopship. 'After a tedious wait, I finally found Dix and five other soldiers, pals of his, slightly under the influence dancing and singing *We'll Meet Again* at the top of their voices. And they *did*, several years later, all suffering from the same serious illness in Churchill House Hospital, Sevenoaks. Alas, all are gone.'

The same song still takes Mrs Alice C. Jones, of Weaverham, Cheshire, back to a night in 1940 'when my husband took my young brother-in-law, aged twenty-four and a pilot in the Fleet Air Arm, and myself to the old Argyle Theatre in Birkenhead. Dickie Henderson was the star and not only he but his twin sisters and his father also, finished the show with that song. We never saw my brother-in-law again, as he was killed piloting a plane which crashed in the Scottish mountains, killing all aboard, including Sub-Lieutenant Tennyson, the husband of Nova Pilbeam, the actress.'

Forty years on, many people still bear the hidden scars of war with all its deaths and disappointments and broken romances.

'Scottie', who prefers to remain anonymous as her husband has neither a forgiving nor a sentimental nature, still thinks wistfully of her lost *Fellow on a Furlough*, whom she met at a wartime dance. 'We met a few times, whenever he was on leave, and of course wrote to each other all the time. Our song, as he called it, was perfect for us, and the times and circumstances. It was perhaps corny, but it meant a lot to us.

'I adored that young man and have never, nor will ever forget him, and the wonderful times we had together. We had everything in common, liked the same things; laughed at the same things. However, he wouldn't let down his school-time girl back home (I'd always known about her). When the war ended he was sent back home. I heard from him until he married. I got married, too, but my husband and I haven't much in common except our family and our years together. I *know* it's not fair to him, but I still think of my lost *Fellow on a Furlough*, even after all these years. I even destroyed all my precious photographs of him, but that didn't help me to forget either!'

For hundreds of thousands of other people there is nothing left but memories and lingering melody which still haunts them to this day. 'I agree with you,' says Mrs Elsie Taylor of Blackburn, Lancs, 'that old songs bring back memories both sad and sweet. Last week on television they played one of my favourites, *I'll never smile again*, which brought back poignant memories of an old sweetheart who was killed at Anzio beachhead.

'Of course, it was only one of the many songs I used to sing with all my heart. Once, I'd gone for a night out with some friends to a pub for a sing-song in a piano room. The pianist started to play *Yours*. I was singing away to my heart's content, when my eyes met those of a handsome soldier across the room. I was just singing the part which goes "I never loved anyone the way I loved you". Before I had finished the next line, he had walked across the room and had given me a lovely kiss.'

Ports and harbours which brought safety and relief to men came to symbolise the sadness of last departures for the women who remained at home. Mrs Brown, of Marsden, South Shields, writes: 'I was courting a Merchant Navy chap and every time he went away, I would go down to the harbour to see him off, and stand, with tears in my eyes, singing *Harbour Lights*. . . . Sad to say he was drowned at sea during the war. Mrs Richards of Northenden, Manchester will always remember for similar reasons *I'll be with you in Apple Blossom Time*, which was originally published in 1920 but which was successfully revived during the war. 'It always reminds me of a Norwegian sailor I met when his ship came to dock in Salford. We were always together each time he came back during

Above and opposite: The moment everyone had been waiting for.

the war. Then the thing people dreaded happened to me. I got a wire "Missing, presumed killed in action". All my letters were returned that I had written on his last trip. He never reached the port where he would have received them. I shall never forget this sailor or our song.'

That best-selling song, *White Christmas*, brings back memories of her brother for Mrs D. Dyer of Wythenshaw.

He was sent out to Burma with the Army. In one of his letters her brother, 'a very gentle and sensitive boy' said that he always felt sad and homesick whenever he heard that tune. Mrs Dyer writes: 'We, his family, always feel very upset when we hear it now, because my brother never came home again.'

Like many other widows and mothers, Mrs Ethel Crook, aged seventy-nine, of Levenshulme, Manchester, still goes 'cold all over' whenever she hears the song *Hometown* which was played on the German radio every Thursday before they announced the names of prisoners of war. She says: 'I sat glued to my chair, waiting to hear if the name of my son, Jack, would be given for he had been reported missing on 24 February 1944. But he knew and I knew as I stood at the doorway waving goodbye on his last leave that I would never see him again—only his grave in the Bavarian Alps.'

Mexicali Rose was the favourite song of Mrs F. M. Dawson of Eccles, and her husband. They were married on 8 March 1944, and had just two weeks together before he was sent to France. 'Like many more boys he never came back; but he left me something very special, his son that he never saw.' For Mrs C. H. Levenshulme, of Manchester, *Begin the Beguine* brings back memories of a very sad time for her family. Her father was dying in hospital just before the blitz on Manchester, when her mother went to the hospital to collect his few possessions. 'She found amongst them a scrap of paper with some of the words of that song written in very shaky handwriting indeed: "To live it again, is past all endeavour."'

But many of the easy hopes of wartime were not to be fulfilled. The majority of people were already too mature and too cynical of politicians to be deluded by any easy promises of 'a land fit for heroes' such as those which had deceived their fathers and their mothers after the First World War; but the true taste of wartime democracy had made them promise themselves a different post-war world, a promise which was given an overwhelming endorsement by the return of a strong Labour government just before the end of the war. Once the enemy pressure was released, however, there was no consensus to prevent the nation from splintering into many separate fragments again. The old dichotomy of 'them' and 'us' had been destroyed in wartime to be replaced after the war by new 'thems' of many different kinds and breeds.

The inability to sustain the spirit of wartime unity and the personal failures to fulfil ambitions conceived in wartime have combined to make the post-war years doubly disillusioning for some individuals, even though most of them are better off today than they have ever been before. But for the majority of English people the war was not fought for materialism so much as the right to live in peace and harmony with others, undisturbed by extremisms of any kind. In spite of all the doubts and disturbances of the post-war years this still remains the hidden ambition of most English people. These hopes are still kept alive in the dated rhythms and the words of wartime songs, with their cheerful message of endurance in the face of all adversity, which still preserve for many people the heroic spirit of other days.

POSTSCRIPT

THE voices with which we ended the last chapter are the authentic voices of ordinary men and women, recalling with little bitterness or self-pity their youthful losses and deprivations for which the earlier moments of happiness snatched from the long years of wartime separation can never fully compensate. Their sacrifices went mainly unrewarded; their thoughts and feelings have also been largely unrecorded until now. Not everyone, of course, remembers the war in this way. Some had less need of popular songs to focus feelings, but without ordinary people's stubborn fortitude, courage and convictions—and, perhaps, the songs which helped to sustain them in their moments of trial—there could have been no victory.

It is easy to be over-sentimental about wartime songs. Behind the smiling faces of the crooners in the dance hall or on the variety stage, there sometimes lurked dark, murderous jealousies of a rival's greater success; some of the most frequently broadcast tunes owed their repetition far less to public acclaim than to the payments of song-pluggers who flourished then just as much as they had done pre-war; while the success of some songs could depend more upon an analysis of the market than on any depth of feeling in the composer or the lyricist. Yet, even though some songs may not have come straight from the heart, like all successful art, popular or more cultivated, they went straight to the hearts of the audience because they had captured their rhythm and their beat.

The popular songs of wartime encompassed far more segments of life than those of pre-war days. There were songs for all seasons and occasions, ranging from the simple patriotic song like *There'll always be an England* to the impudent defiance of (*We're gonna hang out*) *The Washing on the Siegfried Line* whose boast was ultimately fulfilled when advancing Allied armies hung a pair of knickers on the reputedly impregnable West Wall during the closing stages of the European war. The Blitz and the black-out, rationing and romance, separation and Service life were all celebrated—with ironic humour when appropriate—in popular songs. They also charted year by year the changing course and fortunes of the war. These songs helped to bring people together, as they had never done pre-war, in the communal expression of feelings, and in thought, however long and distant the separation. They comforted as they provided assurance of better times to come.

TYPICAL ARMY
MEALS, HOME COMMAND, 1940

BREAKFAST 7.30 a.m.:
Tea, bread and butter, two boiled eggs, marmalade.

DINNER 1 p.m.:
Roast beef, Yorkshire pudding, potatoes and cauliflower,
fruit salad and custard.

TEA 4.15 p.m.:
Tea, bread and butter, jam, rock cakes.

SUPPER 7 p.m.:
Cocoa, sausage, mashed potatoes, bread and margarine.

FOOD RATIONING
(per person, per week)

		Initial ration	Later variations
Jan., 1940	Bacon or ham	4 oz.	4–8 oz.
	Butter	4 oz.	2–4 oz.
	Sugar	12 oz.	8–12 oz.
March, 1940	Meat	1s. 10d. worth	1s.–2s.
July, 1940	Tea	2 oz.	2–4 oz.
March, 1941	Preserves	2 oz.	2–4 oz.
May, 1941	Cheese	1 oz.	1–8 oz.
	Margarine and fats	6 oz.	6 oz.
Nov., 1941	Tinned foods etc.	4 points	4–5 points
July, 1942	Sweets	2 oz.	2–3 oz.

REMEMBER THESE?

1. AA   4. CEMA   7. JPC   10. OTC   13. WAAF
2. ABCA   5. ENSA   8. LDV   11. PLUTO   14. WLA
3. BEF   6. EPT   9. MOI   12. VAD   15. WRNS

(Answers on page 190)

SOME SUMMER SONGS, 1939

MY PRAYER
DEEP PURPLE
IF I DIDN'T CARE
AND THE ANGELS SING
I GET ALONG WITHOUT YOU VERY WELL
BOOMPS-A-DAISY!
SOUTH OF THE BORDER (DOWN MEXICO WAY)
LITTLE SIR ECHO
THE BEER BARREL POLKA (ROLL OUT THE BARREL)
J'ATTENDRAI
CHEROKEE
WISH ME LUCK (AS YOU WAVE ME GOODBYE)

FIRST WARTIME HIT SONGS, 1939

WE'LL MEET AGAIN
KISS ME GOODNIGHT, SERGEANT-MAJOR
(WE'RE GONNA HANG OUT) THE WASHING ON THE SIEGFRIED LINE
THERE'LL ALWAYS BE AN ENGLAND
RUN, RABBIT, RUN!
SING A SONG OF SUNBEAMS
AN APPLE FOR THE TEACHER
MY HEART BELONGS TO DADDY
NURSIE! NURSIE!
THIS CAN'T BE LOVE
GOODNIGHT, CHILDREN, EVERYWHERE
I'LL BE SEEING YOU
LORDS OF THE AIR
SOMEWHERE IN FRANCE WITH YOU

WHOSE SIGNATURE TUNE?

1. SAY IT WITH MUSIC
2. WHEN DAY IS DONE
3. THE SWEETEST MUSIC
4. WHISPERING
5. BUGLE CALL RAG
6. SOMEBODY STOLE MY GAL
7. HERE'S TO THE NEXT TIME
8. IT'S JUST THE TIME FOR DANCING
9. I BRING TO YOU SWEET MUSIC
10. MUSIC, MAESTRO, PLEASE
11. IN THE MOOD
12. SHE'S MY LOVELY

(Answers on page 190)

SOME WARTIME SLOGANS

DIG FOR VICTORY
HELP TO KEEP THE NATION FIGHTING FIT
LEND A HAND ON THE LAND
CARELESS TALK COSTS LIVES
GO TO IT
LEND TO DEFEND THE RIGHT TO BE FREE
COUGHS AND SNEEZES SPREAD DISEASES
SAVINGS STAMPS LICK THE SQUANDER BUG
MAKE DO AND MEND
IS YOUR JOURNEY REALLY NECESSARY?
FOOD IS A MUNITION OF WAR—DON'T WASTE IT
DON'T SPEND—DO LEND
EVERY SCRAP OF PAPER HELPS VICTORY

US HIT PARADE, JULY, 1940

1. THE WOODPECKER SONG
2. SAY IT
3. WHERE WAS I
4. SHAKE DOWN THE STARS
5. IMAGINATION

6. WITH THE WIND AND THE RAIN IN YOUR HAIR
7. PLAYMATES
8. IT'S A WONDERFUL WORLD
9. TOO ROMANTIC
10. THE SINGING HILLS

From the *Melody Maker*, 6 July 1940.

SOME HIT SONGS OF 1940

SO DEEP IS THE NIGHT
I'LL PRAY FOR YOU
TILL THE LIGHTS OF LONDON SHINE AGAIN
YOU'VE DONE SOMETHING TO MY HEART
CARELESS
IT'S A LOVELY DAY TOMORROW
WHERE OR WHEN
TOO ROMANTIC
I'VE GOT MY EYES ON YOU
IF I SHOULD FALL IN LOVE AGAIN
A NIGHTINGALE SANG IN BERKELEY SQUARE
IN THE QUARTERMASTER'S STORES (MY EYES ARE DIM I CANNOT SEE)
IT'S A HAP-HAP HAPPY DAY
IN THE MOOD
SCATTERBRAIN
THE LADY IS A TRAMP
FOOLS RUSH IN
GIVE A LITTLE WHISTLE

FAVOURITE VOCALISTS, 1940

MEN

1. Denny Dennis
2. Chick Henderson
3. Sam Browne
4. Al Bowlly
5. Jack Cooper
6. Leslie Douglas
7. Bob Mallin
8. Sam Costa
9. Dan Donovan
10. Brian Lawrance

WOMEN

1. Vera Lynn
2. Evelyn Dall

3. Celia Lipton   7. Dolly Elsie
4. Anne Lenner   8. June Malo
5. Beryl Davis   9. Gwen Jones
6. Judy Shirley   10. Rita Williams Molly O'Connor

(From a readers' poll published in the *Melody Maker*, 16 March 1940.)

TOP TWENTY BANDS, 1940

1. Ambrose
2. Joe Loss
3. Billy Cotton
4. Oscar Rabin
5. Jack Harris
6. Harry Roy
7. Henry Hall
8. Eddie Carroll
9. Sidney Lipton
10. Ken Jones
11. Carroll Gibbons
12. Jack Hylton
13. Jack Jackson
14. Geraldo
15. Maurice Winnick
16. Billy Ternent
17. Jack Payne
18. Lew Stone
19. Jack White
20. Mantovani

(From a readers' poll published in the *Melody Maker*, 24 August 1940.)

SOME SONGS FROM THE MOVIES

1939

Sing a Song of Sunbeams, Bing Crosby, *East Side of Heaven*.

1940

Over the Rainbow, Judy Garland, *Wizard of Oz*

Isn't that Just like Love, Mary Martin, *Love Thy Neighbour*

Only Forever, Bing Crosby, *Rhythm on the River*

When You Wish upon a Star, 'Jiminy Cricket', *Pinnochio*.

1941

South American Way, Carmen Miranda, *Down Argentine Way*

Our Love Affair, Judy Garland, *Strike up the Band*

It's Foolish but it's Fun, Deanna Durbin, *Spring Parade*

Kiss the Boys Goodbye, Mary Martin, *Kiss the Boys Goodbye*

You Stepped out of a Dream, Tony Martin, *The Ziegfeld Girl*

You Started Something, Betty Grable, *Moon Over Miami*.

1942

I Remember You, Dorothy Lamour, *The Fleet's In*

Don't Sit under the Apple Tree (With anyone Else but Me), The Andrews Sisters, *Private Buckaroo*

How About You, Judy Garland, *Babes on Broadway*

Dearly Beloved, Fred Astaire, *You were*

Never Lovelier
Moonlight Becomes You, Bing Crosby,
Road to Morocco
Tangerine, Bob Eberly and Helen
O'Connell, *The Fleet's In.*

1943

You'll Never Know, Alice Faye, *Hello,*
Frisco, Hello
I couldn't sleep a Wink last Night, Frank
Sinatra, *Higher and Higher.*

1944

Is you is, or is you ain't Ma Baby, Louis
Jordan, *Follow the Boys, Spring will be a*
little Late this Year, Deanna Durbin,
Christmas Holiday.

1945

Suddenly it's Spring, Ginger Rogers, *Lady*
in the Dark
Ac-cent chu-ate the Positive, Bing Crosby,
Here Come the Waves.

US HIT PARADE, AUGUST, 1940

1. MAKE BELIEVE ISLAND
2. I'LL NEVER SMILE AGAIN
3. SIERRA SUE
4. FOOLS RUSH IN
5. IMAGINATION
6. THE BREEZE AND I
7. I CAN'T LOVE YOU ANYMORE
8. PLAYMATES
9. WHERE WAS I
10. I'M NOBODY'S BABY

(From the *Melody Maker*, 24 August 1940.)

SOME SONGS OF THE BLITZ
(September, 1940–May, 1941)

WHISPERING GRASS
I'LL NEVER SMILE AGAIN (UNTIL I SMILE AT YOU)
ALL THE THINGS YOU ARE
BLESS 'EM ALL
ONLY FOREVER
PENNSYLVANIA 6–5000
THANKS, MISTER ROOSEVELT
AIN'T IT A SHAME ABOUT MAME
JUST ONE OF THOSE THINGS
ROOM FIVE HUNDRED AND FOUR
THE LAST TIME I SAW PARIS
I'VE GOT SIXPENCE (AS I GO ROLLING HOME)

A NIGHTINGALE SANG IN BERKELEY SQUARE
ON THE ISLE OF MAY

MORE SONGS OF 1941

YOURS
LET THERE BE LOVE
I CAME, I SAW, I CONGA'D
I, YI, YI, YI, YI (I LIKE YOU VERY MUCH)
RUSSIAN ROSE
WHEN THEY SOUND THE LAST ALL-CLEAR
MY KATRINA
KISS THE BOYS GOODBYE
SAND IN MY SHOES
ISN'T THAT JUST LIKE LOVE
I HEAR A RHAPSODY
YOU STEPPED OUT OF A DREAM
YOU DON'T HAVE TO TELL ME, I KNOW
YOU STARTED SOMETHING
AMAPOLA
HEY, LITTLE HEN!
LONDON PRIDE
IT'S FOOLISH BUT IT'S FUN
WHY DON'T WE DO THIS MORE OFTEN

SONGS OF 1942

THAT LOVELY WEEKEND
I KNOW WHY
WHAT MORE CAN I SAY
MA, I MISS YOUR APPLE PIE
SOME SUNNY DAY
ELMER'S TUNE
THE ANNIVERSARY WALTZ
TANGERINE
SOMEONE'S ROCKING MY DREAMBOAT
DEEP IN THE HEART OF TEXAS
YOU ARE MY SUNSHINE
DON'T SIT UNDER THE APPLE TREE

US HIT PARADE, MAY, 1942

1. DEEP IN THE HEART OF TEXAS
2. I DON'T WANT TO WALK WITHOUT YOU
3. SOMEBODY ELSE IS TAKING MY PLACE
4. MISS YOU
5. BLUES IN THE NIGHT
6. MOONLIGHT COCKTAIL
7. THE WHITE CLIFFS OF DOVER
8. SHE'LL ALWAYS REMEMBER
9. TANGERINE
10. I REMEMBER YOU

(From the *Melody Maker*, 16 May 1942)

MORE SONGS OF 1942

CHATTANOOGA CHOO CHOO
HOW ABOUT YOU
MISS YOU
I REMEMBER YOU
WHEN THE LIGHTS GO ON AGAIN (ALL OVER THE WORLD)
JEALOUSY
WHITE CHRISTMAS
BE CAREFUL, IT'S MY HEART
I'VE GOT A GIRL IN KALAMAZOO
MOONLIGHT BECOMES YOU
SERENADE IN BLUE

US HIT PARADE, JANUARY, 1943

1. WHITE CHRISTMAS
2. PRAISE THE LORD AND PASS THE AMMUNITION
3. MANHATTAN SERENADE
4. WHEN THE LIGHTS GO ON AGAIN
5. DEARLY BELOVED
6. MISTER FIVE BY FIVE
7. SERENADE IN BLUE
8. MY DEVOTION
9. DAYBREAK

10. THERE WILL NEVER BE ANOTHER YOU
(From the *Melody Maker*, 9 January 1943)

SOME SONGS OF 1943

PISTOL PACKIN' MAMA (LAY THAT PISTOL DOWN)
BE LIKE THE KETTLE AND SING
CONSTANTLY
THERE ARE SUCH THINGS
WHO WOULDN'T LOVE YOU
YOU WERE NEVER LOVELIER
I'M GOING TO GET LIT UP (WHEN THE LIGHTS GO UP IN LONDON)
YOU'D BE SO NICE TO COME HOME TO
DON'T GET AROUND MUCH ANYMORE
YOU'LL NEVER KNOW
ALL OR NOTHING AT ALL
THIS IS THE ARMY, MR JONES
JOHNNY DOUGHBOY FOUND A ROSE IN IRELAND
DER FUEHRER'S FACE
COMING IN ON A WING AND A PRAYER
PRAISE THE LORD AND PASS THE AMMUNITION
AMERICAN PATROL

SOME SONGS OF 1944

MAIRZY DOATS AND DOZY DOATS
I HEARD YOU CRIED LAST NIGHT
A LOVELY WAY TO SPEND AN EVENING
LILLI MARLENE
DON'T FENCE ME IN
ROLL ME OVER
I'LL GET BY
IF YOU EVER GO TO IRELAND
TAKE THE A TRAIN
BIG NOISE FROM WINNETKA
A JOURNEY TO A STAR
NO LOVE, NO NOTHING
LONG AGO AND FAR AWAY
SHINE ON VICTORY MOON

MUSICAL FAVOURITES, 1944

DANCE BANDS
1. Squadronaires
2. Geraldo
3. Carl Barriteau
4. Skyrockets

SMALL COMBINATIONS
1. Harry Parry and his Sextet
2. Buddy Featherstonhaugh and his Sextet
3. Stephane Grappelly and his Swingtette
4. Arthur Mouncey and his RAF Band

SOLOISTS
1. George Chisholm (trombone)
2. Carl Barriteau (clarinet)
3. Harry Parry (clarinet)
4. George Shearing (piano)

MALE VOCALISTS
1. Benny Lee
2. Johnny Green
3. Denny Dennis
4. Len Camber

FEMALE VOCALISTS
1. Anne Shelton
2. Doreen Villiers
3. Beryl Davis
4. Dorothy Carless

(From a readers' poll published in the *Melody Maker*, 13 May 1944)

SONGS OF 1945

IT COULD HAPPEN TO YOU
THERE GOES THAT SONG AGAIN
I'M GONNA LOVE THAT GUY
WE'LL GATHER LILACS
COMING HOME
THE MORE I SEE YOU
MY DREAMS ARE GETTING BETTER ALL THE TIME
LOVE IS MY REASON
THE GIPSY

ANSWERS

Remember These: 1. Anti-Aircraft, or Ack-Ack; 2. Army Bureau of Current Affairs; 3. British Expeditionary Force; 4. Council for the Encouragement of Music and the Arts; 5. Entertainments National Service Association; 6. Excess Profits Tax; 7. Joint Production Committee; 8. Local Defence Volunteers (later the Home Guard); 9. Ministry of Information; 10. Officer Training Corps; 11. Pipeline under the Ocean; 12. Voluntary Aid Detachment; 13. Women's Auxiliary Air Force; 14. Women's Land Army; 15. Women's Royal Naval Service.

Whose Signature Tune: 1. Jack Payne; 2. Ambrose; 3. Maurice Winnick; 4. Roy Fox; 5. Harry Roy; 6. Billy Cotton; 7. Henry Hall; 8. Henry Hall (introductory theme); 9. Geraldo (earlier, *Lady of Spain*); 10. Harry Leader; 11. Joe Loss; 12. Billy Ternent.

ACKNOWLEDGEMENTS

I should like to thank the many people who wrote to me to give me their personal song-memories of the Second World War as a result of a letter of mine which was published in various newspapers and magazines. I am particularly grateful to: Mrs Marjorie Ainsworth, Bolton; Mr F. G. Allen, Thorpe, Norwich; Mrs Joyce Ansell, Farnham; Mrs A. Bennett, Northfield; Mrs G. Bennett, Bristol; Mrs Dorothy Boardman, Worsley, Manchester; Mrs Brown, South Shields; Mr Alfred E. Bruce, Moss Side Manchester (ex-BEF, 1939–1943, repatriated POW); Mrs Lilian Cartwright, Swinton, Manchester; Mr Hughie Charles; Mr J. Cocksey, Wyth, Manchester; Mr H. R. Corby, Corby, Northants; Miss N. Coward, Poole, Dorset; Mr T. Coyne, Shaw (ex-33rd Fld Regt, 3rd British Inf. Divn); Mrs Ethel Crook, Levenshulme, Manchester; Mr J. L. Cull, Oldham; Mr R. M. Daniel, Moston, Manchester; Miss Hilda W. Davison, Wolverhampton; Mrs F. M. Dawson, Eccles; Mrs Eleanor Derbyshire, Cheetham, Manchester; Mrs Helen P. Dickens, Corby; Mrs D. Dyer, Wythenshaw, Manchester; Mr Charles A. Edwards, Solihull, Birmingham; Mr Oswald Edwards ALCM, Ruthin, Clywyd; Mr M. G. Edwardson, Altrincham, Cheshire; Mrs Ada Evans, New Moston, Manchester; Mrs G. Farrell, Stockport; Miss Evelyn G. Fiford, Bristol; Mr Edmund Fletcher, Bolton; Mrs W. Gallagher, Solihull, Birmingham; Mr Norman Gardiner, Highfield, Southampton (ex-1156779, LAC, RAF) Mr J. German, Romiley, Stockport; Capt. H. R. Gibbs, Brentwood, Essex (ex-Durham LI); Mrs I. Gibson, Sunderland; Mrs A. M. Glover, Hythe, near Southampton; Mrs Pat Gorner, Millbrook, Southampton; Mrs Helen Grant, Kilmarnock, Ayrshire; Mr Ernest H. Green, Chislehurst, Kent (ex-RAF); Mrs G. Green, Southampton; Mr D. Grindley, Manchester; Mr Bob Halfin, Campbell Connelly & Co. Ltd, music publishers, London; Mr John Harris, Northenden, Manchester; Mrs Hewitson, Blackburn; Mrs May Holbrook, Washington; Mrs M. Holmes, Norwich; Mr W. P. Holt, Sheffield (late Fusilier); Mr Norman Howes, Totton, Southampton; Mrs Winifred E. Hughes, Bramhall, Cheshire; Mrs Iris Hutchings, Knowle, Bristol; Mrs R. Hutchinson, Malton, Yorks; Mrs May Insley, Salford; Mr Ralph Jeffery, Sale; Mrs Alice C. Jones, Weaverham, Cheshire (Weaverham and District Branch Secretary, North-Western Area Treasurer, Women's Section, Royal British Legion); Mr W. A. Jones, Brenty, Bristol; Mrs Joan Kelly, Fallowfield, Manchester; Miss Marjorie Lee, London; Mrs C. H. Levenshulme, Manchester; Mrs M. Lowe, Wyth, Manchester; Mr E. Lunt MM, Bolton (ex-Warrant Officer, RAMC, Secretary, Bolton and District Far Eastern Prisoner of War Association); Miss Edith Lynes, Edgbaston, Birmingham; Mr Donald M. Matheson, Sutton Courtenay, Oxon (Hon. Sec. Sutton Courtenay branch, Royal British Legion); Mr Albert McGrath, Avonmouth, Bristol; Mr N. D. Moore, Oldbury; Mrs O. Morgan, Horfield, Bristol; Mrs M. V. Morton, Kings Norton, Birmingham; Mr Denis Murray, Littlemore, Oxford; Mrs J. Nessworthy, South Shields; Mr William Gilbert Parry, Swinton, Manchester (ex-Army 3536189); Mr A. G. Pittar, Crondall, Farnham (ex-WO 74504); Mr Les Porteous, Manchester; Mrs Gladys Rawsthorn, Bolton; Mrs R. Richards, Northenden, Manchester; Mr S. Rigney, Hyde, Cheshire (ex-11th LF); Mrs Sheila Roberts, Costessey, Norwich; Mrs A. Rogers, Birmingham; Mr George W. Self, Alton, Hants; Mrs Nancy Mavis Senior, Whitchurch, Bristol; Mrs Peggy Smith, Wolverhampton; Mrs Winifred M. Snowden, Sinnington, York; Mrs Alice Solomon, Brandon, near Durham; Mrs Bett Spridgeon, Whittlesey, Peterborough; Miss Jean Stanhope, Fulford, York; Mrs U. Stares, Swaythling, Southampton; Mrs Jean Stokes, Northallerton, Yorkshire; Mrs Esmé Strachey, Iping, Hants; Mrs Elsie Taylor, Ramsgreave, Blackburn; Mrs Doris Thompson, Garstang, near Preston; Mr John Trickett, Edinburgh; Mr Samuel Turnbull, Glasgow; Mrs G. Tyszkiewicz, Kingstanding, Birmingham; Mr F. C. Wadsworth, Swindon (ex-Sapper 11415498, HQ, No 2 Rly Constr. and Mtc Group, RE); Mr Clifford Walker, Kidderminster; Mrs Walters, Oxford; Mrs Agnes Wearden, Blackburn; Mr Leonard Western, Sheffield; Mr Stan White, Kettering; Miss Hilda May Whorton, Wombourne, near Wolverhampton; Mrs M. Whyatt, Reddish, Stockport; Mrs Alice E. Wilby, Warstock, Birmingham; Mrs Nell Wild, Bewdley, Worcestershire; Mrs Hilda M. Withenshaw, Kingsley, Cheshire; Mr G. Wood, Prestwich, Manchester (ex-RO); Mrs Joan L. Worrod, Great Barr, Birmingham.

My special gratitude goes to Mr Ted Platt, of Belper, Derby, who was so enthusiastic about the project, that he took the trouble to write a long detailed history of his own experiences of the war, only parts of which I have been able to use for reasons of space. I am also deeply grateful to Terry and Shirley LeGoubin, Mac and Pauline Millington, and my wife Ren, who all helped me greatly in my search to find the most appropriate title for this book.

I should also like to thank the newspapers and magazines which put me in touch with most of the people named above by publishing my letter, especially the *Birmingham Evening Mail; Bolton Evening News;*

ACKNOWLEDGEMENTS

Bristol Evening Post; Chester Chronicle; Choice Magazine; Derby Evening Telegraph; Eastern Evening News, Norwich; *Edinburgh Evening News; Farnham Herald; Glasgow Evening Times; Huddersfield District Newspapers; Lancashire Evening Telegraph*, Blackburn; *Leeds Evening Post; Liverpool Echo; Manchester Evening News; Northern Echo*, Darlington; *Newcastle Evening Chronicle; Northampton Evening Telegraph; Oxford Mail; Peterborough Evening Telegraph; Royal British Legion Journal; Sheffield Star; Shields Gazette; Southern Evening Echo*, Southampton; *Sunderland Echo; Swindon Evening Advertiser; Wolverhampton Express and Star; Yorkshire Evening Post*, York. I should like to thank Mr N. Brooks, Postbag Editor, *Manchester Evening News*, and Mr James Gray, Features Department, *Edinburgh Evening News*, who made special efforts on my behalf.

The editor of *Melody Maker* kindly allowed me to quote the results of several readers' polls published during the war. Popular newspapers and magazines still provide one of the most valuable records of wartime life: I am grateful to all those named in the text.

Transcripts of Crown copyright records in the Public Record Office appear by permission of the Controller of HM Stationery Office. I have used WO 163/247, WO 32/11194, WO 32/11477, all on Morale and Welfare in the Far East; Inf. 1/260, letter and memo from Sir Kenneth Clark; Inf 1/284, Director-General of Post Office on Morale; Lab 26/44, letter from Mr Charles J. Bartlett.

Some of the background reading which was most useful in writing the book is included in the bibliography below.

SELECT BIBLIOGRAPHY

Robert S. Arbib Jnr., *Here we Are Together, The Notebook of an American Soldier in Britain*, Longmans, 1946.

Asa Briggs, *The War of Words, The History of Broadcasting in the United Kingdom*, Vol 111, Oxford University Press, 1970.

BBC Year Books, BBC, 1939–45.

Angus Calder, *The People's War*, Cape, 1969.

Sid Colin, *And the Bands Played On*, Elm Tree, 1977.

Billy Cotton, *I did it My Way*, Harrap, 1970.

Basil Dean, *The Theatre at War*, Harrap, 1956.

Ralph Ingersoll, *Report on England*, John Lane, The Bodley Head, 1941.

Alan Jenkins, *The Forties*, Heinemann, 1977.

Norman Longmate, *How we Lived then*, Hutchinson, 1971.

Vera Lynn, *Vocal Refrain*, W. H. Allen, 1975.

Albert McCarthy, *The Dance Band Era*, Studio Vista, 1971.

Brian Rust, *The Dance Bands*, Ian Allan, 1972.

George T. Simon, *Glenn Miller and his Orchestra*, W. H. Allen, 1974.

Sunday Pictorial, *Sweethearts All*, Hutchinson, 1945.

The author would like to thank the following for their kind permission to reproduce the songs:

Francis, Day & Hunter Ltd. for 'I'll Be Seeing You' © 1938 by Chappell & Co. Inc. (USA).

Peter Maurice Music Co. Ltd. for 'A Nightingale Sang in Berkeley Square', 'Lilli Marlene' © 1944 by Appollo Verlag (Germany) and 'Yours © 1932 by E. B. Marks Music Co. Ltd. (USA)

B. Feldman & Co. Ltd. for 'The White Cliffs of Dover' © 1941 by Shapiro Bernstein & Co. Inc. (USA)

Noel Gay Music Co. Ltd. for 'Hey Little Hen' words and music by Ralph Butler and Noel Gay.

Dash Music Co. Ltd. for 'There'll Always be an England', and 'We'll Meet Again'.

Chappell Music Ltd. for 'Kiss Me Goodnight Sergeant Major' Music and words by Art Noel and Don Pelosi © 1939 Bradbury Wood Ltd. and 'That Lovely Weekend' Music and Words by Ted and Moira Heath © 1941 by Bradbury Wood Ltd.

Southern Music Publishing Co. Ltd. for 'You Are My Sunshine' by Davis and Mitchell, and 'Der Fuehrer's Face' by Wallace.

Campbell Connelly & Co. Ltd. for 'Goodnight Sweetheart'

Cavendish Music Company Ltd. for 'The Quartermaster's Stores' by Box, Cox and Read.

Keith Prowse Music Publishing Company Ltd. for 'Roll Out The Barrel' © by Shapiro Bernstein & Co. Inc. and 'Bless 'Em All'.